Advance Prai

Solace is a must-read for the bereaved, as well as for social workers and psychologists. This is the only book a mental health professional needs on their grief-counseling shelf. Written with Dr. Temes's characteristic compassion, *Solace* takes the reader through the entire bereavement process in vivid detail. I will hand this book to my patients as homework and as a jumping-off point in our sessions in their grief recovery.

—Renee Garfinkel, clinical psychologist
practicing in Washington, D.C.

Solace offers hope for recovery. Dr. Temes writes with such warmth, kindness and comfort, offering permission to grieve in whatever way works for you. You will not only embrace Dr. Temes's advice, you will also love hearing the voices of many men and women who have experienced a significant loss. Dr. Temes talks to you like a good friend, so you will not feel alone when *Solace* is beside you.

—Ingrid Schweiger (DrIngrid.com),
psychologist practicing in Massachusetts

Solace

Finding Your Way Through Grief and Learning to Live Again

Roberta Temes, Ph.D.

American Management Association

New York • Atlanta • Brussels • Chicago • Mexico City • San Francisco
Shanghai • Tokyo • Toronto • Washington, D.C.

Special discounts on bulk quantities of AMACOM books are available to corporations, professional associations, and other organizations. For details, contact Special Sales Department, AMACOM, a division of American Management Association, 1601 Broadway, New York, NY 10019.
Tel.: 800-250-5308.   Fax: 518-819-2372.
E-mail: specialsls@amanet.org
Website: www.amacombooks.org/go/specialsales
To view all AMACOM titles go to: www.amacombooks.org

This publication is designed to provide accurate and authoritative information in regard to the subject matter covered. It is sold with the understanding that the publisher is not engaged in rendering legal, accounting, or other professional service. If legal advice or other expert assistance is required, the services of a competent professional person should be sought.

Library of Congress Cataloging-in-Publication Data

Temes, Roberta.
    Solace : finding your way through grief and learning to live again / Roberta Temes.
        p.   cm.
    Includes bibliographical references and index.
    ISBN-13: 978-0-8144-1463-7 (pbk.)
    ISBN-10: 0-8144-1463-X (pbk.)
    1. Grief.   2. Bereavement—Psychological aspects.   I. Title.

    BF575.G7T454   2009
    155.9'37—dc22

                                        2009009839

Printing number

10   9   8   7   6   5   4   3   2   1

Dedicated to the memory of my parents,
Eleanor and Irving Rempell

Contents

Author's Note

This book is for you if someone you love has died. This is a book of comfort. I understand how difficult it is for you to constantly see that empty chair, that empty place.

Solace: Finding Your Way Through Grief and Learning to Live Again will help you get on with your life. For decades, I have counseled people going through bereavement, and their experiences are reflected in the advice I offer you. Also, the latest scholarly research is very much a part of the psychological guidance presented here.

You *will* get through this. You *will* get on with your life. It won't be the same life you had. It will be your life with a new perspective.

Tens of thousands of readers were helped by my previous book about bereavement, *Living with an Empty Chair*, which was a best-seller. The soothing tone of this book is the same as that one, but this book has the benefit of thirty more years of research and a twenty-first century viewpoint.

While preparing this book I asked many former clients, friends, and family members for advice for you as you proceed through your bereavement. Some offered brief tips, while others told long stories. I have placed these heartfelt words for you throughout the book. I hope you find them helpful.

Read the chapters in any order you wish. Some chapters may help you today and others may not seem relevant to you for many months. You will benefit from *Solace* by reading those pages that call to you; for now, don't worry about the other information. This is a book of comfort. You will refer to it over and over.

Acknowledgments

I appreciate the efforts of my extraordinary agent, Janet Rosen, at Sheree Bykofsky Associates, Inc., as well as the efforts of the hardworking editors at AMACOM Books—Jacquie Flynn, Erika Spelman, and Jennifer Holder. I appreciate the efforts of my clients, colleagues, and friends who generously shared their stories. You've eased readers' bereavement journeys. Thank you.

Introduction

You are experiencing this death in your unique way. Your experience is valid for you. Your response is right for you. Your way is the right way for you, for now. Don't let anyone suggest that you are mourning the wrong way. You are your own expert.

Trends come and trends go. Philosophies are in vogue and out. Stop listening to bereavement experts; they will change their minds and what is considered abnormal today will be obligatory tomorrow.

For example, there was a time when experts claimed that you must talk about the death, cry about the death, wail about the death. You were instructed to go directly to a psychiatrist if you were unable to loudly express your grief.

Today we know better. I am here to tell you that the death of a loved one is not a mandatory trauma that prevents you from functioning. You can handle this ordeal, painful as it is. You will cope with the death in the same manner you have coped with other difficult situations in your past. If you come from a family of stoic people, you will probably suffer quietly and then get back to your regular routine. The absence of outward signs of distress may be your typical coping style, an indication of your strong spiritual outlook, or simply the way in which your family handles a crisis.

Here is what Elaine said soon after the death of her much-beloved husband, to whom she was married for forty-two years:

"I allowed myself to cry and feel sorry for myself for a few days and then I said, *Enough.* I looked forward and didn't look back. It's been three years now since he died and I feel okay and my life is progressing. Of course I think about Don, but only for a few minutes here and there. And even then I think only about the good days, before he got sick. I refuse to allow myself to think of those bad, dark days at the end of his life."

Somehow Elaine has been able to pull this off. Some of her relatives think she is hard-hearted. Some of her friends think she is not telling the truth. Elaine insists that she can actually stop herself from reminiscing. She says that in her past, whenever there were troubles in her life, she had the ability to block them out of her mind. And that method of coping works for her.

> ✿ *Suggestions from a Neighbor*
>
> *Keep your loved one's address book. My mother's telephone/address book is the greatest inheritance I have from her. I love seeing her handwriting and reading the names of all the people she was involved with—everyone from doctors to neighbors to the dressmaker. It's been many years since she's gone and I still feel good whenever I look at that book.* ✿

Whatever works to make life bearable at this time is what's right for you. Steve told me that when his wife died, he threw himself into his work. His extended family wondered why he didn't visit them more often. They wanted to feed him and to talk to him about his beloved wife. His friends wondered why he didn't show up for their weekly basketball games. His boss wondered why he was working late into the night and on weekends, too.

Steve said, "I was afraid that if I stopped I would crack up. So I just kept going. I rarely spoke to anyone. Finally, about five months after Madeline passed away, I felt strong enough to talk about her, or at least to mention her name."

According to researchers, mourners who avoid confronting their loss and do not speak about their feelings recover from their bereavement at the same rate as the mourners who process and work through all their thoughts and feelings.

Countless survivors of unspeakable tragedies have managed to endure precisely because they refused to speak about their ordeals. Often, after decades, these people finally felt emotionally protected from their painful memories. And that is when they began to speak about the traumas they had lived through—be it witnessing a murder, surviving a rape, escaping from the Holocaust, or enduring a childhood of physical or sexual abuse. Sometimes, silence gives strength.

Similarly, if your family is a family of wailers I suspect your mourning cries will be heard by many, and then you, too, will return to your regular routine. Loud volume is part of the bereavement process for you.

Whether you avoid talking about it or loudly shout it, or choose a style of expression that is in-between, your grief exists. Your grieving style makes no difference when it comes to your recovery. You will recover. Think about the way you were before the death, before that final illness if there was one. That is the state you will return to when you finish grieving. And I promise you, you will finish. Of course, even when grieving is over, you will still have strong sad feelings, but the day-to-day intensity will be diminished.

Please ignore the folks who insist that if only you tried harder or if only you put your mind to it, you could feel better instantly. They mean well but they are misguided. They are akin to the folks who insist that if you "think positive" you can cure cancer. Positive thinking is wonderful. It can help you cope with a situation and it may help you regard the situation in a new way. It may even boost your immune system. However, it does not change the situation. Sadly, your loved one is still gone.

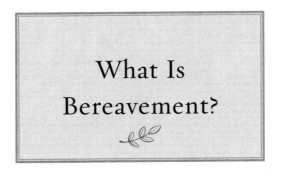

CHAPTER I

What Is Bereavement?

After a death, you go through a normal life crisis and like any other normal life crisis you need a period of adjustment. We call the period of adjustment after a death *bereavement*. Bereavement is a process. It is a healing process. Bereavement is the state of sorrow you feel after a loved one is gone and that state encompasses both grief and mourning.

Grief is your emotional response to the loss. What you experience in your mind and in your body is your grief response. Grief reactions seem automatic and beyond your control. When you sob or scream or huddle under your bedcovers, you are expressing your grief. Grief symptoms alert others to your situation; everyone you encounter is thus reminded to treat you gently. Most of your grief reactions will occur when you are alone; grief is a private experience. Comfort yourself by knowing that your grief reactions are a continuation of your love.

Mourning describes the things you do because you are grieved. The actions you take during mourning are determined by the social, cultural, and religious groups to which you belong. Mourning actions are planned actions, as opposed to the spontaneous emotional outbursts of grief. When you say a particular prayer or when you decide to stay home rather than go to a dance, you are following mourning rituals.

Bereavement is a psychologically necessary state. Whether you react with anger or with numbness is not the point. The point is that you are reacting and it is normal and necessary for you to do so.

Adjusting to a death is particularly difficult if you had no preparation for it. In the past, when something new was coming up in your life, you prepared for it. Prior to marriage comes engagement, which is a period of adjustment. Prior to parenthood, there is a pregnancy, another period of adjustment. When moving to a new neighborhood, you anticipate reaching out to community institutions to help you adjust. After accepting a new job, you learn about the culture of the new workplace. All these transitions, even though prepared for, create difficult emotional adjustments. Each bride, new dad, new neighbor, or new employee, at first, feels unsure when assuming the new role. Uneasy feelings are expected and are simply part of that period of adjustment.

And so, too, it is with bereavement. Possibly, you never prepared to be without your loved one and never imagined what it would feel like. Bereavement is your period of adjustment. Bereavement is the process that helps you adjust to your new state—the state of living with that empty chair.

Someone you loved has died and you are going through a normal life crisis. Powerful emotions may emerge. Fear of becoming overwhelmed may appear. Pain may surface. And still you must go on. Even though you are bereaved, you are expected to continue with your responsibilities, your chores, and your life. It is necessary for you to take care of yourself. It is necessary for you to go on living even though that chair is still empty. Not an easy task. But you *can* do it. You will do it.

RENEE'S STORY

I was twenty-two years old with a new baby when my father was diagnosed with lung cancer. We had been extremely close and he was gone in six weeks. I wasn't yet over his death when two years later my twenty-eight-year-old husband was diagnosed with terminal cancer.

I wish somebody at hospice would have told me that certain signs—blue feet, labored breathing—meant the end was imminent. I had no clue and thought those symptoms were just part of the illness.

I was not prepared for the true sadness and shock I felt. And I was not prepared for the anger I had toward others who still had a father and still had a husband. I'm fifty years old and I still feel that my father abandoned me.

I don't feel abandoned by my husband because within two years of my husband's death I remarried the perfect man for me.

If I had it to do over again, I would have waited to get rid of their personal effects and taken my time to choose what I wanted to keep.

I think there should be sensitivity training for how to care for the caregivers. I was exhausted all the time but people kept asking how my husband was, not me. All the focus was on my husband, but I was working eight hours a day because we needed the health coverage, and I was arranging for child care, taking care of everything and everyone. Those were dreadful days for me.

As you begin your trek through bereavement, you may wish for a temporary separation from the world. Most religions have a prescribed number of days when you are required to observe rituals and abandon your daily obligations. Many employers offer bereavement leave. Take advantage of these opportunities.

Even though death has physically removed your loved one from you, please understand that the relationship still exists. You cannot eliminate a deep attachment. It remains. And that is a good thing.

You are not alone. The U.S. Census Bureau of Vital Statistics keeps track of the way we die and when we die. The bureau notes that the average life expectancy of Americans is rapidly nearing eighty years old. That's the good news. Yet, whenever someone does die, there is a mourner. That's the sad news.

According to the U.S. Census Bureau, there are almost 12 million widows and 2.69 million widowers in the United States today. Almost half (43 percent) of all women age 65 and older are widows. By the time a woman reaches age 85, and these days many, many women do reach that age, fully 79 percent are widowed.

Your loved one may have died because of an age-related illness, or from cancer, of AIDS or from the complications of diabetes, of murder or from suicide, or perhaps from an infection he picked up in the hospital. Your loved one may have died while defending our country in the armed forces or after being hit by a drunken driver. Or, your loved one may have slipped on a patch of ice, as did Dr. Atkins of diet fame, or he may have been killed by fireworks or by botulism, or perhaps a heart attack or stroke did him in.

Sooner or later every life comes to an end. And it is the survivor who is left with the empty chair. Rich or poor, young or old, no one is exempt from feeling grief. All mourn. All suffer.

Your loved one, thankfully, has left you with memories. You have the memories of shared activities, and also the memories of a shared life. The hopes and dreams, the perceptions and ideas, the habits and viewpoints of your beloved are still yours to access. That is a good thing. The chair is still empty, but your memory bank is full.

> 🌿 *Suggestions from Barry, a Widower*
>
> *The more I looked at photos, the more my memories came back. I remembered the trips we took and the events we attended. Although the pictures made me cry a lot, they also made me realize what a full life we shared. Take out your scrapbooks and photo albums and remember to print out any photos you have on your computer or in your phone.* 🌿

Some philosophers have opined that true love might be proved by wishing to outlive your loved one. In that way, the person you love will not have to suffer the anguish of grief. Grief is tough. Grief feels as if it will break your heart.

INITIAL NUMBNESS

Countless documents have been written to explain what you should be feeling today and what you should be feeling next week and next month, too. Please ignore all such advice. *Your* time frame is the right time frame for you.

Amitai Etzioni, the well-known professor and sociologist, wrote an op-ed article for the *New York Times* after his young-adult son died. That untimely death occurred soon after the death of Etzioni's wife in a car crash.

> There seems to be an expectation that after a great loss we will progress systematically through the well-known stages of grief. . . . My family, close friends, and I keep busy. . . . We try to avoid thinking about either the immediate past or the bereft future. . . . I presume that many a psychiatrist and New Age minister would point out that by keeping busy we avoid "healthy" grieving. To hell with that. The void left by our loss is just too deep.

Bereavement typically includes three distinct stages: initial numbness, disorganization, and reorganization. But, some people may spend two days in stage one, a month in stage two, and then go on to the final stage; while others are in stage one for many months and stage two for several years. Such variations are normal and many people vacillate from stage two to stage three over a long period of time. Your stage one may be very different from your neighbor's stage one. These stages are just broad, general outlines of a typical bereavement period.

Usually, the first stage is characterized by feelings of numbness. Simply getting through the day is an accomplishment.

LARRY NEWMAN'S STORY

My father's death was totally unexpected. How does a person prepare for disbelief? My father died on a Saturday night. He and my mother were playing poker at a friend's house. My father was usually unlucky in cards. Finally, he won a hand. As he reached over to pull in his winnings, he looked at my mother and collapsed. He suffered a massive myocardial infarction and instantly died.

My father was my best friend and I still, after all these years, want to pick up the phone and share some news with him. Work was the best therapy for me. Also therapeutic was helping my mother and other family members. I was the person to make the funeral arrangements and designated to be the mature, level-headed one.

Although it has been more than thirty years and I am a grandfather today, I still suffer over the death of my father because I miss him so much. My suffering now is not about mourning but rather about a feeling of emptiness. My tower of strength crumbled way too soon.

This stage of emotional numbness begins at the moment of death. If you are fortunate, you have friends and family around you and they will provide food and comfort and car rides and telephone numbers. Afterward, you may not remember what they've done for you because during this time you are in somewhat of a daze. You may feel as if you are suspended in an unreal state. You may not even be able to grasp the full significance of your loss. Maybe you are thinking you're in the middle of a bad dream and soon you'll awaken.

You may notice that you are maintaining an emotional distance from the devoted folks who are helping you. That's exactly how it should be. You have to do so much and arrange so much that you cannot let anything interfere with your tasks. If you stop to get close to your loving helpers, your feelings might emerge and overpower you.

Instead, this is the time to concentrate on discharging the immediate chores having to do with the funeral, banks, lawyers, and more. You may feel as if you are functioning in an automatic, robotic way. That's good; it helps your mind protect you from fully recognizing the painful finality of death. You'll be better prepared to confront reality after a bit of time has elapsed.

If you are overwhelmed by the number of people who are calling you, simply put a general message on your answering machine. Let callers know that you appreciate their attentiveness but you won't be able to return their call for several weeks. This gets you off the hook for now, and you need only respond to those who will be most helpful to you at this time. Eventually, you'll get around to speaking to everyone. Eventually, you will want to speak to everyone. For now, though, your primary responsibility is to yourself.

This stage may last for just a couple of weeks or it may last for many,

many, months. Soon, you may feel worse. Ironically, that is progress. When you feel worse, it's because the next stage of bereavement is making itself known.

> 🌿 *Suggestions from Cheryl in Oregon*
>
> *I took to bed and didn't get up for two weeks. My kids ate from the refrigerator or maybe at their friends' houses. I really don't know. It took me two weeks to be able to face the world. Not that it's easy now. My father was my everything and now I miss him more than words can say. Hide out in your room is my advice. I know it helped me.* 🌿

DISORGANIZATION

You know you are entering the next stage of bereavement when the insulation provided by shock is wearing off; your haze is lifting. And, sadly, the family members who were so attentive to you are now back pursuing their regular lives, and the friends who were so solicitous to you have likewise resumed their former commitments. You feel alone. People who phoned you daily might now be calling only once a week.

Joyce reported that after her father passed away, she didn't need to cook for ten days because each evening a full dinner magically appeared on her doorstep. Neighbors organized and volunteered and made sure she had food and wouldn't need to bother shopping or cooking. "But," said Joyce, "during those early days I had no appetite and everything was one big blur. The next few weeks were wretched times when I could barely push myself to the supermarket. I sure could have used some home-cooked food then."

It seems that for everyone but you life has returned to what it was before the death. This does not help you. Ironically, it is now that you could benefit from closeness; you no longer need that emotional distance. You are actually feeling your loss, feeling a void. There is acute loneliness and emptiness where once there was life. Please be reassured that these horrible feelings are totally normal, appropriate, and expected during this phase of bereavement.

This is the time when friends, neighbors, and relatives may become alarmed about you. ("She was taking it so well, but now look at her. Could she be having a breakdown?") That's because during this period of disorganization many of your symptoms are the symptoms of depression. You may have shortness of breath and the need to frequently sigh. You may feel fatigued and perhaps have tightness in your throat. Your sleep habits and eating habits probably are not the best right now. This is all to be expected during this second stage of bereavement.

> 🌿 *Suggestions from Alice in Brooklyn, New York*
>
> *I was helped by reading my husband's boring accounting books. They would put me to sleep on the nights when I thought I wouldn't be able to sleep. And I kept them on my night table for when I would wake up during the night. They always did the trick. So my advice to you is to get some boring books.* 🌿

Your Emotions Now

You are in despair and when people are in despair they feel bleak about their future. They are aimless and apathetic. You may wonder, "Where is my enthusiasm, my drive, my passion for life?" Don't worry. Your true personality will return; you just need some time.

It is normal, at this stage, to feel a full range of emotions. You can feel strong and yet vulnerable; sad, but sometimes happy; lonely for companionship, yet sometimes hostile toward certain people—even people who are trying to help. Sometimes a mourner will lash out at a helper for no apparent reason. Has this happened to you? If so, don't worry. This is a fleeting part of stage-two bereavement.

Sometimes rage surfaces and you may shock yourself by directing that rage toward people you don't even know. You may be angry at strangers just because they are alive and your beloved is not. And you may be angry at your loved one for having died. Yes, you know it's not your loved one's fault, but nevertheless you've been abandoned. In your disorganized state you may ask, "Why me?" Strong feelings are proof of your humanity and of your attachment to the deceased. If a stranger had died your feelings would be faint, your reactions tepid.

William Shakespeare gave recognition to the fury of the bereaved in *King Henry VI* when he wrote: "We mourn in black; why mourn we not in blood?"

Other emotions expressed during this middle phase of bereavement may include shame, dread, panic, or helplessness. C. S. Lewis's book *A Grief Observed*, begins with the sentence, "No one told me that grief felt so like fear."

Some people feel guilty during this time. You may feel guilty because you are experiencing relief. If your loss occurred after a long illness then even though you miss the person, a part of you feels relieved because your physical responsibilities have ended. You can now leave the house without worrying. You can sleep through the night without dread. It is okay to simultaneously feel devastation and relief.

Becky, a new widow, said, "These past six months were unbelievably frightening. I never knew which of those seizures or falls would kill him. I barely slept, I lost twenty-seven pounds, and I almost lost my sanity. I loved him deeply until the end, but I am so relieved that it is over."

Are you feeling guilty because of words you spoke to your loved one? Please know that if you have a deep and meaningful relationship, you do have the luxury of sometimes shouting, resenting, and perhaps even saying, "Drop dead." Those words, spoken in anger, reflect a close relationship. Harsh words are proof of shared intimacy. You would never speak to a stranger with such intensity. Your words neither caused nor hastened the death. You do not have magical powers. If you did, you'd use those supernatural talents today to whisk you right through to the end of bereavement.

Strangely enough, if you had a difficult relationship with the deceased, you may be experiencing more upset than if your relationship was smooth. When the person with whom you had some issues is gone, there is no way for those issues to ever be resolved. While he was alive, you had hope for a resolution and for a good relationship. Now there is no hope.

Agnes came to my office for a consultation. Her mother had died about three weeks earlier. Agnes was puzzled by her response to the death. She asked,

"Dr. Roberta, why am I so upset? I saw my mother once a year, at Christmas, and I thought that was too often. She was not a good mother in any sense of the word. I left home when I was 18 and never looked back. So why am I weeping in your office at age 36? I didn't even like her, and yet I can't sleep at night and can barely keep myself together at work. What's going on with me?"

I explained to Agnes that as long as her mother was alive she had hope—hope that they could have a decent relationship, hope that her mother would change, hope that they could talk about their past. But now none of that is possible. Agnes was suffering because she had lost more than her mother; Agnes had lost her hope.

Cliff came to my office several months after his beloved wife passed away. I had known Jeanne from the neighborhood and saw the deterioration that occurred to her ill body during the past year. Cliff cared for her day and night. Jeanne outlived her original prognosis, which predicted she'd be gone in three months. She lingered for seven months.

Cliff said, "I loved my wife so much. We were together since high school. She was my best friend and the closest person to me. What's wrong with me, Doctor? I haven't cried and I'm not skipping a beat—just doing my life as always. I go to work and I chat with my colleagues as if nothing is wrong."

I explained to Cliff that he had already done much of his mourning. *Anticipatory grief* is a normal reaction to loss and it begins before the death. People begin mourning the loss of the simple pleasures of life that they can no longer share with their loved one. During that time of serious illness the process of bereavement begins, and thoughts about the future without the loved one run rampant, even while the loved one is still alive. Cliff remembered that months earlier, before Jeanne died, he had a difficult time at work and would often get choked up when speaking to his staff.

When the death is preceded by anticipatory grief, it's likely that your mourning will follow a different path than if you did not have all that time to prepare for the inevitable ending. Cliff had several months in which to make funeral arrangements, enlist the aid of friends and family, think and plan for the times ahead, and imagine what life would be like without Jeanne. During those months, he had shed plenty of tears while balancing all the demands of running a household, caring for a terminally ill wife, and working his regular job. Cliff's course of bereavement is unique for him, just as your course of bereavement adapts to your particular situation.

Are you feeling sorry for yourself? Self-pity is often a necessary component to grief. Don't worry; you will pity yourself less as time goes on. You might still ask, "Why me?" but you won't spend so much time trying to come up with an answer. Instead, eventually, you will once again engage in life.

The distinguished actress Helen Hayes, when asked to comment on her adjustment to widowhood, candidly admitted, "For two years I was just as crazy as you can be and still be at large. It was total confusion. How did I come out of it? I don't know, because I didn't know when I was in it that I was in it." Sometimes feelings of bereavement are so overwhelming that mourners, like actress Helen Hayes, do not realize how disorganized and discombobulated they are until a fair amount of time passes and they can look back at themselves with some objectivity.

Dr. Joyce Brothers, the preeminent psychologist, wrote about her feelings after the death of her beloved husband in her book *Widowed*. She said, "I maintained my lecture schedules, made television appearances, wrote my columns, flew back and forth across the country but it was all on automatic. The zest was gone."

This stage of bereavement is painful—and even more painful if you were dependent on the person who died. How dependent were you on the deceased? Did you depend on your loved one to provide you with encouragement? With understanding? With money? With meals? With conversation? With everything?

The more ways in which you needed and depended on your beloved, the more you will feel your loss. Whether it's changing the baby's diaper or changing the flat tire, balancing the checkbook or carving the turkey, you will feel upset when you are compelled to do a chore that someone else used to do for you or with you.

Feelings of abandonment are quite common during this stage of bereavement. Willard Gaylin, a psychiatrist at Columbia University, has said, "If you feel you needed the other person in order to cope with life, then they threaten your very survival by dying and you feel abandoned."

My neighbor Helen was overwhelmed after the death of her dear husband of many decades. She had little to worry about; her husband had left a full portfolio of stocks and bonds. The bank accounts were brimming, too. Nevertheless, Helen felt her husband had abandoned her. She would now have to make decisions about investments. She never before did that; it was her husband's job. She would now have to make decisions about accountants and financial advisers. This, too, was always her husband's domain. Helen did not want to learn any of this, and yet it was her new responsibility. She needed her husband and felt deserted and neglected by him.

Bereavement may be particularly difficult for you if you were totally defined by the role you played in your relationship with your lost loved one. If your daily routine was all about responding and reacting to your loved one's needs, this is an extremely difficult time for you. Gradually, you will begin to live your life according to your needs. This will take time.

Not only have you lost your loved one, you've also lost your partner in certain activities. Does this death deprive you of a role you enjoyed? It's possible you have lost an important position. Perhaps now you have no one to cook for or no one who depends on you for advice or for money or for going out to the mall. Maybe there's no one to laugh at your jokes or to comment when you sing in the shower. It is normal for you to feel that emptiness.

During this middle phase of bereavement, life seems frightening and complicated. Daily tasks become monumental. The layer of psychological protection developed during the initial stage of bereavement has diminished. This is the time when you may be feeling sorry for yourself and your predicament. Sorrow for oneself is an appropriate and universal feeling at this point in time.

This is the time when desperate mourners do rash things that they may regret. Newly widowed people who were long-married may be so desperate to be held and to feel another body next to their own that they invite strangers into their home or they commit themselves to inappropriate relationships. My friend Naomi, upon being widowed, figured out a wonderful way to be close to a man, be held by a man, and then be able to walk away unscathed at the end of the evening. She joined a local dance studio. As a side benefit, Naomi became an acclaimed tango dancer!

When he was widowed, Harry, a client, said, "After all these years of marriage, my body aches for the touch of a woman. I don't mean sex necessarily. I just feel like I cannot live without my skin being touched." Harry was helped when he booked a few sessions with a professional massage therapist.

Please don't worry. You will soon finish with this stage and move on to a place of security and safety. You will once again feel at home in the world.

For now, it is normal for you to feel worse than you did immediately after the death. Instantly, after a calamity or emergency, your adrenalin gets you to do what must be done. Your grief response is put on hold while your determination provides strength for you. With the passing of time, your adrenalin dissipates and your determination withers and you feel your true feelings. It hurts. But, the hurt will lessen; I promise.

Some mourners feel terrible for a year or two after the death, although many observers wouldn't know it. The majority of bereaved people, while still very sad at one month after the death, are able to resume functioning at that time. They still weep but not all day long. Many actually feel proud of their coping ability at this time. Do you?

Some bereaved people report that during the first year after the death, their thoughts tend to be negative. They think of the final illness or accident. They think of the sadness or the shock of it all. Mourners may accentuate the negative traits of their loved one soon after the death. This is a natural phenomenon and occurs most often when the last year(s) of the deceased's life was very different from all previous years. The negative thinking does go away—but it takes time.

Here's what Debbie said about her negativity:

"I urge other widows to think about the good years when they reminisce. Don't do what I did at the beginning and think about the years of sickness. My husband was ninety-two and I was in my seventies when he died. He was sick for five years, so I knew I would lose him and his death was not a shock. In fact, it was a relief because he was not himself during those last years. He was a problem both mentally and physically. Prior to his illness, he was never a problem and always a joy. We had been very close. Now I've learned not to let myself think about those last five years. Instead, I think about all of the other years. They were the good years. Our earlier life was very happy and full of fun. That's what I remember now when I think back. That was my Joe."

Remarkably, after about a year, negative thoughts and feelings are extremely rare. Your mind just doesn't go there anymore. Instead, you find that you are thinking about earlier times and happier events. This change in thinking seems to occur by itself, as if the mind is saying, "Enough, already, let's get on with life."

B.R.'s Story

My mother was sixty-nine when she died. I knew she was very sick and when I returned from visiting her in Florida, I decided to put things in order in my business and then fly down and stay with her until she recovered.

During the night before my flight down, I suddenly awakened and sat bolt upright in my bed. I later learned that was the moment my mother had a stroke. But I didn't know that then and I went to the airport and landed in Florida thinking she was the same as when I left her earlier in the week. I called my sister from the airport and she told me she couldn't pick me up because mom was in the hospital and gravely ill.

I had a very slow taxi driver and I did think of beating him over the head, throwing him out of the car, and driving myself to the hospital. Good thing I didn't know the route; I might've done it.

I would have been helped during the illness and afterward if I had known about Elizabeth Kübler-Ross's book, *On Death and Dying*. If

I had known the information in the book at my last visit before mom's death, I would have talked to my mother about what she probably knew. We could have shared the process of dying by talking about it. It would have been easier for both of us.

It's been thirteen years and I am still bereaved. The only thing that helps a little is when a new baby is born into the family. With each birth some of the sadness lifts.

Your Needs Now

If you are having a difficult time now, please know that it is normal to suffer, feel overwhelmed, and wonder when you will get back on track. You also may be wondering what you can do to help yourself. Here are some ideas:

• *You need to talk about your life with the deceased.* If you find yourself repeating the same stories just give yourself permission to do so. You simply need to articulate certain memories. You may wish to inform your friends and family that this need will not last too long, but for now you'd appreciate it if they will listen to you as you review all aspects of the relationship. Your memories are important and sharing them will warm your heart.

• *You need to talk about the circumstances of the death.* It may be necessary for you to reiterate every last detail about that fateful day. Such recounting is good for you. As you relive those last few hours, your mind comes to recognize the reality of the death. Again, apprise others that this need to speak almost obsessively of particular incidents is temporary. People who love you will patiently listen as you recount that same story many times. Soon, your need won't be so urgent and you'll no longer want to report these tales.

• *You do need proper nutrition.* If your appetite is suffering, try to fill yourself with soup and with ice cream and take a daily multivitamin with minerals. Often, it is too much effort to figure out what to eat and then too difficult to actually chew your food. Soup slides down, so does ice cream. Eat them until your appetite returns. When people who care about you ask what they can do for you, suggest having a meal together. Your appetite may perk up when you are not alone with your food.

• *You need sufficient sleep.* Sleep is restorative and every cell in your body benefits when you get a good night's sleep. Establish a nightly ritual that will help you sleep. Perhaps a warm bath, maybe a calming conversation, or possibly some soothing music will help. To enhance falling asleep, stay away from caffeine and stay away from bright lights before bedtime. Use a task light, not an overhead light, in the evening because bright lights can act as stimulants. If you awaken during the night and have trouble falling asleep again, have something handy that will lull you back to sleep—maybe a gentle CD to listen to, or a glass of water, or a favorite photo to look at. Please consult your medical doctor if sleeplessness persists. You deserve a good night's sleep.

• *You need to be reassured that your symptoms are not dangerous to your health and that your sleeplessness, loss of appetite, and depressive symptoms will soon leave.* It's true; some symptoms of the middle stage of bereavement resemble some symptoms of mental illness. The difference, of course, is that indications of mental illness do not permanently and spontaneously disappear, whereas your grief symptoms will soon be eradicated. If you were not mentally ill prior to the death of your loved one, you will not be mentally ill once you recover from bereavement. The death will not make you mentally ill.

REORGANIZATION

Time passes. Soon, the worst is over. You are now in the final stage of bereavement. You notice that your feelings are less intense. You're not crying as much. Upon awakening in the morning, your first thoughts are not always of the deceased. When falling asleep at night, your last thoughts are not always of the deceased. You notice that many times during each day you are comfortable and calm. You are at ease with yourself.

Maybe a few months have passed since the death, maybe a year, maybe two. You will go through bereavement according to your own timetable, not mine nor anyone else's.

You can recognize the end of bereavement by noting that you are less involved in your past and you are becoming more interested in your future. You will never forget your loved one. He or she will always be part of your life. It is wise to maintain your attachment and preserve your bond. Good memories are crucial to a good life. You will honor those memories, and at the same time you will be committed to continuing on your own path through life. Death has made you aware of the value of life. Please cherish every day.

🌿 *Suggestions from Vivian in Maine*

I made a mistake by putting my daughter's pictures in every room of the house. It made me feel good to look at them and it assured me that we would never forget her. But my other kids' friends were freaked out and didn't want to come to our house. Finally, one of my son's friends told him why he wasn't coming to hang out. So then we put the photos all in one upstairs room and the house was full of friends again. 🌿

The goal of bereavement is not to sever your attachment to your beloved. The goal of bereavement is not to end the relationship. The goal is to weave your precious memories into your life in a helpful fashion. You and your deceased beloved have a relationship that will persist. And now you'll find yourself thinking more about the person's life than about his or her death. You will enjoy the comfort that comes from thinking sweet thoughts about your relationship and you will continue the relationship in your own way.

🌿 *Suggestions from Lorraine, Remarried and Happy Again*

If you lost a spouse, my advice is don't wait too long to find another one. You need to love someone and you need to be loved by someone. You can keep loving a dead husband or wife and also love a live one. I'm doing it and it works well. 🌿

(Text continued on page 24)

Dr. Temes's Overview

Stage of grief	Duration	Characteristics
STAGE ONE: Numbness	Several weeks or months	Insulation Mechanical functioning
STAGE TWO: Disorganization	Many, many months	Sleep and appetite difficulties Sorrow for oneself Painful feelings Depression Loneliness
STAGE THREE: Reorganization	Several weeks or months	Occasional peacefulness Feelings less intense

of the Grief Process

Needs	Developmental Task	Helper Functions
Emotional distance	To protect self from feeling impact of loss	To assist with chores
Intimacy, Expression of feelings	To acknowledge impact of loss	To listen
Encouragement to reenter life's mainstream	To accept the loss	To expand the bereaved's social network

During this final stage of bereavement you'll begin, once again, to have some fun. You have a right to paint the kitchen or to buy a new car or to laugh at a colleague's joke. And certainly it's time to get away for a few days, if at all possible. If you are lucky, there are people in your environment who will reach out to you and encourage you to reenter life.

This is the time to look for people or community institutions that will help you expand your social network. Join a political discussion group, book a cruise, enroll in a French class, sign up for bridge lessons, reconnect with Cousin Nancy, and go to the gym, too. The world has been diminished because of the loss of your loved one, but you are no longer diminished; you are emerging from your grief.

When you reach this point, you deserve congratulations. Bereavement is a long, hard journey. Finding your way through grief and learning to live again is an achievement worthy of praise.

CHAPTER 2

Cause for Concern?

Feelings and behaviors that occur during bereavement can seem extreme and sometimes scary. In addition, there are people attempting to tell you how you should be mourning your loved one and how you should be getting on with your life. You are in distress, you are experiencing some emotions you have never before experienced, and you may sometimes wonder, "Am I normal?"

WHEN TO WORRY

How do you determine if you are within the realm of normalcy or if you may be developing a more serious emotional condition?

In psychological studies, the people who at two months after the death are still in extreme distress and not yet functioning at all need some outside help. In fact, it is these very people who, if they don't get help, usually in the form of antidepressant medication, tend to remain somewhat impaired in their functioning for years.

Bereavement happens to an existing personality. You have your strengths and your weaknesses, and life has already given you some experience in coping with loss. Certain individuals, more than others, are extremely vulnerable to the stresses of bereavement. Find out if you are among those who are at risk for extra suffering by answering these questions.

In the past have you suffered from:

- Major clinical depression?
- Generalized anxiety disorder?
- Panic attacks?
- Severe responses to a previous loss?

If you answered yes to any of the these questions, your brain knows how to react in a troublesome fashion. Many people reexperience the strong, traumatic feelings of previous deaths when they are confronted with a new death. This *cumulative grief* is extremely painful and may create a more difficult bereavement path for you.

It is wise to look at yourself carefully and decide if you might be suffering from what is called *complicated grief*. Complicated grief is sometimes called *pathological mourning*. Pathological, in this phrase, simply means excessive. Complicated grief is diagnosed if several months after the death you are experiencing the following symptoms:

• *You have developed obsessions about the deceased and cannot think about anything or anyone else.* You'll notice that even when you are with other people, you cannot concentrate on the conversation. Your thoughts remain focused on your beloved.

• *You refuse to face the fact that the person has died.* At first, it may be normal to exclaim, "I can't believe he's gone." Later on, though, you should be able to articulate the following sentence: *I know that _____ is dead.* If you still cannot believe he is permanently gone, you'll live your life exactly as you did when he was with you. You plan as if he is with you and you speak as if he is with you. You do not engage in activities because you are waiting for him to join you.

• *You continue to yearn and search for the deceased.* You are restless and cannot find a comfortable place for yourself. You are nervous because nothing interests you except the idea of reuniting with your beloved.

- *You cannot resume your regular functioning because of your persistent pain of loneliness.* Even when you are with other people, you feel lonely. You may be tempted to drink or abuse drugs to get out of your misery. It's too difficult for you to work or take care of your responsibilities.
- *You perpetually feel stunned that the death could or did occur.* Even if the death may have been unexpected and untimely, after a while you should be able to talk about the deceased without shock.
- *You have deep feelings of emptiness and impending danger.* If you are going about your daily life feeling that "the other shoe is about to drop," that feeling is indicative of serious anxiety.
- *You are losing too much weight and are in danger of developing malnutrition.* The ability to chew your food and develop an appetite usually returns after several weeks.
- *You cannot sleep at night.* Your body needs to rest and your mind needs to rest. You need your sleep in order to have the strength to get through bereavement. Bereavement is not easy. Sleeplessness is a significant symptom and must be addressed.

Scientists at UCLA recently used MRIs to investigate complicated grief. They determined that in a small number of bereaved people, thoughts of the deceased activate an area in the brain that should not be activated. It is the part of the brain called the nucleus accumbens.

So, if you have complicated grief, whenever you think about your deceased loved one, you get excessive feelings of pleasure in your brain. Those feelings are so excessive that they are similar to the feelings an addict gets when using an addictive substance.

Now you know why it becomes almost impossible to stop thinking about your loved one. How can you attempt to live without your beloved when you receive constant pleasure by thinking of him to the exclusion of thinking about anyone or anything else?

With complicated grief, your brain craves the repeated feeling that occurs whenever you think of your deceased loved one. This brain situation prevents you from adjusting to your new circumstance. Your coping ability is nonexistent and you cannot adapt to nor accept your loss. Recurrent pangs of intense longing consistently pop up. Medication becomes a welcome necessity. Without medication, yearning is established as a regular part of daily activity and life cannot move forward.

If you have developed complicated grief, you need medical attention. If your general practitioner or internist or family doctor is experienced in working with bereaved people, you'll get the proper medication. If your regular doctor lacks such experience, make an appointment with a psychiatrist who will know precisely what medication is right for you.

When you get the attention that you deserve, you'll be much stronger and your coping ability will return. You will smile again. Bereaved people tend to have a prompt response to antidepressant medication, which can immediately restore appetite and sleep.

CAN YOU DIE OF A BROKEN HEART?

Researchers who study how our actions, thoughts, and social environments influence our immune system are called psychoneuroimmunology (pronounced *sigh ko noo row imm you no low gee*) researchers. These scientists tell us that it is not being bereaved itself that causes medical problems. Rather, it is the change in your circumstance and your behavior that may cause medical problems for you. For example, if you lose your spouse and now must live alone, it is the social isolation that may be harmful to your health. Or, you might not be eating properly and that could exacerbate diabetes or a heart condition. Or, you might be drinking alcohol to numb yourself and that could exacerbate a tendency toward alcoholism. Or, you might not be sleeping enough and that could make you prone to accidents or illnesses. For all these reasons, you need to check in with a physician if you think you have a case of complicated grief. With the right medication and the right psychological support, you will soon be feeling much better.

Statistics tell us that newly bereaved people go to the doctor more often than those who are not bereaved. We used to think this meant that the death of a loved one caused a survivor to get sick. We now believe that increased visits to a physician usually occur because of the following reasons:

- Prior to the death the survivor was busy caring for the sick patient and had no time to go to the doctor for himself or herself.
- The survivor now knows how important it is to obtain good medical treatment.

So, you will not die of a broken heart. Family support and social support lessen grief responses. The more involvement you have with family members and the more social ties you have, the easier your bereavement will be. Yet, even those who are bereaved and have no support manage to survive and eventually live well.

Sometimes one spouse follows another in death. That is not because one death hastens the other. There are situations where a couple consists of two very elderly people, and statistically the elderly do die. There are situations where both spouses had similar risky habits—perhaps smoking, overeating, or not taking their prescribed medications. Those habits tend to promote death.

All the latest scholarly studies say that there is not an increased death rate for the bereaved. Should you come across an old study that "proves" that there is, just ignore it. If all widowed people died soon after their spouses died, we would not see 12 million widows in the United States and nearly 3 million widowers. Nor would we have throngs of bereaved parents filling meeting rooms, seminars, and websites with their terrifying tales.

STRANGE THINGS ARE HAPPENING

Sometimes, during this difficult time of bereavement, you may feel as if your brain is playing tricks on you.

Are You Having Visitation Dreams?

Visitation dreams seem like visits from your loved one. During your first months after the death, the dreams may be of illness or whatever it was that caused the death. Later on, though, the dreams usually reflect a lighter and happier time.

You will see your beloved in your dream and he will be alive. Perhaps he'll be much younger than when he passed away, or perhaps he'll be as he was. Often such dreams are in bright color and show plenty of action.

Many bereaved people look forward to the night so that they can experience a visitation dream. In some cultures, visitation dreamers believe they are in touch with the spirit of the deceased. For most Americans, though, these dreams help to maintain their connection with the deceased. The dreams are proof that the relationship endures, even after death.

Are You Having Flashbulb Memories?

Flashbulb memories are memories of a specific important event that are as clear as if they were photos on your brain. You will always remember details of certain incidents. You may remember precisely where you were and what you were doing when you heard about the terrorist attacks on 9/11. If you are older, you may remember where you were when President John F. Kennedy was assassinated. And now, you probably have flashbulb memories of the death or your response to it. You won't have to search your brain for information about the death because the memories are as clear as snapshots.

Author Ann Hood in her book *Comfort* recounts a flashbulb memory of her grief response after the death of her daughter:

> At first, grief made me insane. . . . That is me making that sound which is both inhuman and guttural and the most human sound a person can make: the sound of grief. . . . That is me running, zigzagging, trying to escape what is inescapable: Grace is dead.

As Hood demonstrates, it is perfectly normal and appropriate to clearly remember your extreme response to a hideous circumstance.

Are You Having Hallucinations?

Do you think you hear the footsteps of your loved one? Do you smell his aftershave lotion? Do you hear your deceased child calling your name? Do you hear your mother's voice? If you so desperately want to hear your deceased husband's car pull into the driveway, you probably will hear it one sad day. It's normal to occasionally "forget" that the dead person is permanently gone. The hallucination helps maintain the feeling that your loved one is nearby. Some days you need that feeling. Reports of ghosts and of successful séances may be attributed to the urgent need to be close to the deceased. This is nothing to worry about.

Are You Forgetting About the Death?

Some of your behavior is propelled by habit. You are so accustomed to interacting with the person who is gone that sometimes you continue those interactive habits. The widower, alone in his home, upon hearing the phone ringing shouts, "I've got it, hon." He is simply repeating a habit of decades. Also, the widow who erroneously sets the dinner table for two is repeating a habit of decades.

According to statistics, for the first few months after the death of a spouse, the surviving mate often embarrasses herself when she realizes she is looking for him in a crowd. This habit, too, goes away.

🌿 *Suggestions from Judy in Georgia*

My tip is do not stop talking to her just because she died. I love talking to my mother every day. Of course I know she is gone, but talking as if she is in the car with me on the way to and from work makes all the difference. It makes it possible to go into the office and do a good day's work. When you keep talking, you keep connected. 🌿

🌿 *Suggestions from Arnie in New Jersey*

My advice is when you leave your house put on the television. That way when you return you won't hear the silence and you will have something to distract you right away. 🌿

llistrmm

ARE YOU CRYING?

Tears heal. They are a symbol of strength and a testament to love lost. Remember, only strong people dare to love deeply. Interestingly, emotional tears remove chemicals that build up during times of stress. Animals produce tears that lubricate their eyes, but it is only humans who produce emotional tears that remove toxic substances. That's right—your tears help your body. Crying reduces the body's manganese level, which is a mineral that affects mood and is found in great concentration in tears. Researchers have concluded that when tears remove chemicals built up by the body during stress, the stress level is lowered. It's been proved that suppressing tears increases stress levels. So, please give yourself permission to weep. Keep a box of tissues handy in every room of your home and in your car, too.

Tears in front of others, or in any public place, will quickly elicit nurturing. When you need a hug, remember that crying is an effective method of communication. Bereaved families bond when they all cry together. Men are sometimes accused of being insensitive because they usually cry less than do women. Please understand that men and women show their hurt in different ways. Women talk and weep. Men prefer to take action. They may punch a wall or punch a ball. When they do get around to weeping, though, they report that they feel better.

Maimonides, the brilliant medieval philosopher, said, "Those who grieve find comfort in weeping and in arousing their sorrow until the body is too tired to bear the inner emotions."

During the middle phase of bereavement, you will gain some control of your weeping. You may find it helpful to designate a particular place and a particular time for crying. For example, knowing that you will cry after dinner in the living room may help you hold in your tears during the workday. Some people allow themselves to cry on the weekend but not during the week. Others weep only in the shower, when no one can hear, or only in the car, when they are alone.

Allen, a high school student, came to my office with his mom. Both were recovering from the unexpected death of Allen's dad. Allen asked me if I thought he was "immature, and maybe crazy, too." When I asked why I would think that, he replied, "Because I still need to cry even though so many months have passed. Every night as I am falling asleep, I bury my head in my pillow and cry and cry." What Allen didn't know was that his mother waited until he fell asleep and then she, too, cried into her pillow. She did not want to alarm her son with her sobs.

Allen would have benefited from knowing that Mom, too, needed to weep. It would have normalized his situation. If you are crying, you can be pretty certain that others in your family are crying, too. Let them know about your tears; crying need not be done in secret. There is no shame in tears.

In ancient Rome, mourners filled small, decorative glass bottles with their tears and then placed those bottles in tombs, to be buried with the deceased. This was their way of showing respect and showing love. In fact, it was said that the most important people were buried with the most tear bottles.

Psalm 56:8 in the Old Testament of the Bible suggests that God notes our tears and in that way keeps a record of our pain and suffering. David prays by saying, "Put thou my tears in Thy bottle; are they not in Thy Book?" The idea of collecting tears is clear here and the bottle referred to is probably a water flask.

During the Victorian era, fancy tear bottles were lined up in mourners' homes. The bottles were considered appropriate decorations during the time of solemnity. Supposedly, when the liquid in the bottles evaporated it was time to stop mourning.

Some United States Civil War stories mention wives who cried into tear bottles and then saved all the bottles until their husbands came home from battle.

You might enjoy collecting tear bottles or having one or two at your bedside or displayed on a shelf. If you wish to fill them with tears that's just fine, but it is not necessary. You might just want to have them in your home, as beautiful works of art, and whenever you look at your tear bottles, you'll be reminded that crying is good for you and crying is expected.

Tear bottles today, sometimes called tear catchers or tear vials, are created by artists using fine glass. You can order your own tear bottles from www .solaceafteradeath.com.

> *Suggestions from Marion, a Dog Lover*
>
> *My pets saved my life. When I couldn't pull myself out from under the covers for anything else, I did for my pets. I recommend you get a pet or two or borrow one from a friend or neighbor.*

ARE YOU SUFFERING FROM STRESS?

We know that stress, which used to be called nervousness, occurs during and after a difficult experience. And the death of a loved one is a very difficult experience. We also know that when stress continues for too long a period of time, it may weaken the immune system. It's not good to be chronically stressed. So, to make your bereavement easier and to be sure you are not vulnerable to illness because of a weakened immune system, you must break the cycle of stress in your body. You can do this by using medication and/or you can do this by all the proven methods of stress reduction. These methods include:

Rest

Music

Yoga

Poetry

Friendship

Talk therapy

Vacation

Exercise

Sunshine

What will be your method of restoration?

🌿 *Suggestions from a Widow in Milwaukee*

Take something to make you sleep. Don't tough it out. When I finally agreed to try the sleeping pills that my doctor had been telling me about for six months, they made a very big difference. Sleeping is too important to miss. I can cope much better when I have a good night's sleep. I still cry but I feel a little more hopeful. 🌿

🌿 *Suggestions from Leora in New York*

Somebody should have let me know that it was okay to laugh and to have fun. I felt disloyal if I attempted to have a good time or if I watched anything other than the History Channel and C-Span. I didn't think I had the right to laugh or do anything lighthearted. My advice to you is force yourself to do things that make you laugh. Once you do you will feel better even if it's just for a little while. 🌿

RITA HORA'S STORY

It was twenty-five years ago and I was working at my job in a New York City law office. Suddenly, for no reason, I began to weep. Probably twenty times during that day I broke into tears. I would stop myself and couldn't imagine why I was tearful. Also, I couldn't imagine why I had the urge to call my family in New Delhi, India. We didn't speak that often in those days before cell phones. I repeatedly picked up the phone, started dialing, but then hung up.

It was a relief to get home to my husband and children. But then I had an image in my mind that was peculiar. I saw my mom walking someplace then not getting there because she was turning to look at me over her shoulder. It was as if she was trying to tell me something.

Early the next morning, before the kids left for school and before my husband and I left for work, the phone rang. Of course, it is always bad news at that hour. My mother had died. By that afternoon, I was on a plane to New Delhi.

When I returned to New York, I was a robot and could only function mechanically. I cried every day. I was unable to smile. Nothing helped me until a friend gave me a book. It was a religious book. It taught me about God and it taught me how to pray. For a while I was obsessed with religious books and read them all the time. They definitely made a difference.

The other thing that made a difference was my dream life. My dreams were vivid and real. In one dream, my mother was there right in front of me and she started singing. The words of her song told me it was time to stop crying and reassured me that she was at peace. I still remember the song. It went like this: "If you keep on crying, I cannot rest in peace. I am very peaceful where I am now. It is beautiful here." After a few of those dreams, I was able to believe her and do what she asked.

One day, I just said to myself: "I am allowing the dead to make me neglect the living. I must take better care of my husband and my children. My mother is gone. She will never return." Once I said those words, I was able to follow that advice.

When my father died just a few months after my mother, I already knew about the importance of prayer for me and I could more easily turn to God. I also was helped by finding wise, older people to talk to.

When my father died, my mother came into my dreams again. Although she never knew how to drive, in my dream she was driving a car and my father was sitting next to her. There was a JUST MARRIED sign on the car. They were both smiling and told me they were happy so I should not cry for them.

When they were both gone, I started watching the movies that both of my parents had enjoyed and listening to their music, too. I looked through the photo albums obsessively.

It took a year, going through the four seasons, for me to able to enjoy the memories and not have that strong yearning feeling. My mother continues to visit me in dreams and give me good advice.

CHAPTER 3

Helping Yourself

What can you do to feel better? Sometimes you need to take action. When you do something to relieve your feelings and to give yourself a sense of achievement, you are accomplishing your journey through bereavement. Here are some activities—and some behaviors you can do—that are therapeutic for you during your bereavement.

WORK IS THERAPY

If you are lucky enough to have a job, return to it even if just on a part-time schedule. The structure of getting up and out, the obligation to greet fellow workers, and the need to keep yourself together for a requisite number of hours is good for you. If you do not have a job, this is the time for you to volunteer at the animal shelter, at the local daycare center, or at the hospital gift shop.

After her husband died, Ginny stayed home. She was accustomed to staying home. She had cared for Joe for the two years of his illness. But by staying home, she faced that empty chair all day long. About six months after the death, Ginny's adult son arranged for her to care for Carol, a woman on his street. Carol was recovering from a car accident and needed a helper with her at all times. The helper who had been hired wanted a few hours off each day and that's where Ginny came in. Here's what Ginny reported after her first three weeks on the job:

> "How did I stay in all those weeks? Why did I stay in all those weeks? I love getting out and feeling useful. Carol can already walk with a walker and I helped her get to this point. We watch TV together and play cards. I can't believe I'm getting paid for this. When I get home I'm tired but it's a good feeling of tiredness, not one that comes from being bored. And I noticed that I don't cry for Joe much anymore, although I do talk about him a lot to Carol."

SOCIALIZING IS THERAPY

It's important for you to be among people. Lack of contact with friends and acquaintances is a predictor of difficulty in bereavement. There are probably folks who do not want to intrude in your life at this time and are deliberately staying away. If you are feeling isolated, then it's wise to get in touch with those folks who are being too polite. Set up a lunch date, a weekend walk, or a shopping trip. Adopt a new social policy and say "yes" whenever you are invited anywhere.

Joe is a single guy whose mother, his only relative, died. Joe took my advice and agreed that for one month he would accept all invitations. Here is his report to me:

> "You wouldn't believe it, Doc. I've been to a ball game, the race track, and a two-year-old's birthday party. I ate Chinese food, Mexican food, and Japanese food. I went to a concert and I went to a wake. All because I said 'yes.' I have to admit it beats sitting in the house and looking at mom's empty chair. My heart is still in pieces, but it's different now. I see a future."

ORGANIZING IS THERAPY

When life threatens to overwhelm you, it feels good to have control over something—even if that something is just a room, a desk drawer, a closet, or a shelf. Get yourself back under control by organizing one area of your home at a time. This is a good opportunity to figure out what to do with your loved one's belongings. Many people are helped when they bring all of the loved one's items, objects, and clothes into one room. The rest of the house becomes easier to navigate and that one special room is your "work in progress." Over the next few weeks or months, you can consolidate things in that room, give away what others can enjoy, and eventually have all personal effects in certain boxes, drawers, or shelves. When you need the feeling of closeness to your beloved, you'll know just where to go.

While sorting through items, take the time to decide what you want to keep for yourself. It is helpful to choose some transitional objects. A transitional object is the adult form of a security blanket. It is something that gives you that familiar, cozy, comforting feeling. Select something that belonged to or represents your loved one.

One of my clients sleeps wearing her husband's socks. Another carries her deceased child's report cards in her pocketbook. A young man who lost his fiancée in a car accident wears a ring made out of her engagement ring. You'll feel better when you know you can wear or touch or be comforted by a transitional object. You may have used a transitional object even before bereavement. Do you carry photos in your wallet or do you keep family photos on your desk? Photos of your loved ones are transitional objects. They give you feelings of security; they remind you of home.

🌿 *Suggestions from Dave in Washington, D.C.*

I couldn't bear to clean out my father's desk. I cleaned out everything else in the apartment but I couldn't do that. If you have a similar situation, my tip to you is do what I did. I took a huge lawn-and-leaf plastic bag and emptied everything that I couldn't go through into that bag. I put it in the bottom of my closet and two years later I finally had the guts to go through it all. I'm telling you that there is no hurry, so you can do things when you feel stronger. 🌿

TAKING ACTION IS THERAPY

This can be your time to take action. Maybe you want to inform people about health insurance issues that were an obstacle for you. Maybe you want to persuade your political representatives to advocate for legalization of a particular drug or treatment. Or, perhaps you'd like to create a place to meet with others who suffered a loss similar to yours.

In 1980, thirteen-year-old Cari, the daughter of Candy Lightner, was killed while crossing a street. The driver of the car that hit her was drunk. He had three prior convictions for drunk driving and was out on bail from a recent hit-and-run. Candy felt an intense need to stop drunk driving. Fueled by her urgent rage, she began a group whose mission was to prevent underage drinking and to stop drivers from getting into their cars if they were drunk. Today, you probably are familiar with the organization MADD (Mothers Against Drunk Driving) that Candy Lightner founded. Recently, the group has added a new mandate to its mission: MADD now provides bereavement help for families.

In 1993, on an evening rush hour commuter train, a deranged passenger walked up and down the aisles shooting randomly with a 9mm handgun. Among the victims were a father and son, returning to their Long Island home. The father died from his injuries. Carolyn McCarthy, the new widow, cared for her son who was gravely wounded and thought about that gun. She felt called to action and decided to run for a seat in Congress. Prior to her widowhood she had no political ambitions. But now she had a cause—it was gun control—and she was angry and she ran and she won. Her personal tragedy propelled her to take action.

There are folks who begin websites, chat rooms, or organizations and foundations to highlight a cause that needs consideration. If you wish to draw attention to the circumstances that led to the death of your loved one, or if you wish to educate people about those circumstances, this is a good time to do so. You'll be helping yourself at the same time that you'll be helping others.

FOOD IS THERAPY

Nourish your body properly and it will be good to you. Use mealtime as a social event and invite neighbors and friends to join you. Plan ahead so that you will have company at meals. Get together with others for Sunday brunch, for Wednesday dinner, or for a midweek lunch at a restaurant.

Take the time to look online or in cookbooks for interesting recipes. Find one recipe that looks appealing and practice it and then master it. This can become your signature dish that guests will look forward to. Do you have any homeless in your town? Give them something to eat.

My neighbor Hal felt too depressed to eat after his wife died. When some of us on the street noticed his weight loss, we decided to take turns stopping in at dinner hour and bringing some goodies with us. He was too sad to go out of his house. Then, after a couple of weeks, Hal felt well enough to accept dinner invitations. For a few evenings each week, he could be found at one or another of the neighbors' homes. During this time, a son of one of the neighbors had a high school assignment that required him to teach something to an adult. He decided to teach Hal to cook soup. What a hoot! And these days Hal invites *us* over for meals. Food therapy helped him through bereavement.

> 🌿 *Suggestions from Judith in New York City*
>
> *Dealing with death is humbling. It taught me the limits of what I can control, possess, have, and hold. I have no more illusions or defenses and my true vulnerability is exposed. The support group I attended was a joke and of no use at all. Listening to music unglued my emotions. Sometimes when I tried to work, I just stared at my computer and had a hard time pulling my brain together. I am grateful to the friends who took me out for meals and listened to me talk on and on.* 🌿

PLANNING IS THERAPY

Use a calendar to make your plans. Plan when you will go somewhere new. Plan when you will buy yourself a new outfit. Plan to learn to knit and decide when you'll go to the yarn store. Plan to go fishing and call a buddy who likes to fish. Or, learn how to frame a favorite photo and plan when you will venture to a craft shop or to an art supply store. Plan to repair something in your house and plan to go to Home Depot or to Lowe's or to your local hardware store. Planning activities for your future will help you reach that future.

RELIGION IS THERAPY

Rituals help during bereavement. Investigate what your religion has to offer. What does it recommend a newly bereaved person do? Try it and if you find solace, do continue. If you think it's a waste of time or if it gets you too upset, then speak to your clergyperson and see what else you can do, in the name of religion, to help yourself. Seek out clergy; they are there to help you in bereavement even if you are not a member of their congregation or, even in many cases, their faith.

> 🌿 *Suggestions from Mel in Denver*
>
> *It would have made my life much easier if I was religious. My advice is to get religion in your life. Every person in my bereavement group who believed they would be reunited with their loved one had an easier time than all of us sophisticates who had no religion.* 🌿

There are many useful aspects of religion for the bereaved. There's the joining of voices in song, the praying, the person of authority telling you that you will be helped, the regularity of meeting times, the social component to the service, and the comforting words in religious readings. A believer will find solace in religion.

Some believers become nonbelievers after a death. If you belong to this latter category, please think about attending services anyway. You might derive some pleasure from the process even if you are angry at God. You might find yourself drawn into a discussion with a clergyperson who will help you find your way.

WRITING IS THERAPY

Putting your thoughts and your feelings into words will help you. Writer Sherri Mandell says that daily writing helped her get through that first terrible year after her son was killed. She remembers, "I would just write and cry and write and cry. It was my therapy."

There are many useful writing exercises, for example:

• *Write about the last few days of your loved one's life and then go on to write about the day of the death.* Say everything. Remember all the details and write them.

Here is what Charlotte wrote about the death of her mother:

CHARLOTTE'S STORY

I was home with the baby. He was napping and I was folding laundry and the television was on in the background. When the phone rang I had no premonition. My father was on the line and that was surprising. It was my mother's job to talk to me by phone. Dad just would say "hi" if he answered whenever I called, and then he'd give the phone right to mom. But I wasn't too suspicious that anything was wrong. I actually thought he might be calling to find out how his first grandchild was coming along. Dad said only a few words: "Come here. Your brother is on his way." And then he hung up!

I called my brother. There was no answer and I didn't have his cell number. I lived about forty-five minutes from my parents' apartment. I quickly got dressed, packed a bottle and some diapers, and got in the car with the baby. I called my husband at work to tell him where I was going.

An hour later I walked into their building and my husband was standing in the lobby, apparently waiting for me. I couldn't figure out what was going on. He took the baby from my arms and came upstairs with me.

There were people in the apartment. I didn't recognize all of them. The bedroom door was closed. I asked, "Where's Mom?" A reasonable question I thought. As soon as I asked, everybody started crying and my husband hugged me tight. But nobody told me where she was. Before I got my answer two police officers barged in. My father spoke to them and I heard him say some words: "headache," "nap," and "couldn't rouse her."

Before anybody could stop me, I ran into my parents' bedroom. There was my beautiful mother. Just lying on her bed. I felt relieved. There was nothing wrong. Mom was napping.

The police and my father and my brother came into the room after me. The officers said, "Sorry for your loss, ma'am."

And then I got it. I don't remember much after that. I think I fainted. The next thing I remember I was on the living room couch and my husband was talking to me.

Charlotte told me that after she wrote this account, she read it over and over and then started calling people and reading it to them. She needed the repetition to clarify what happened. This is an important way to process a traumatic event.

Here is what Phil wrote about the death of his wife:

PHIL'S STORY

I knew the death was coming because she was accepted into hospice. I thought I was prepared, but when she started that irregular breathing I didn't know what to do. I called the hospice nurse and she came over right away. She sat on the bed with Marie and spoke to her. I was of no use. I actually went into the kitchen to make coffee. It was too hard to be in that room with them. I wanted to get some coffee, but I couldn't remember how to make it. Part of my brain was saying, "Your wife is dying. Go be with her." But the other part of my brain was saying, "This is too hard to take. Run away."

I think the nurse must have called my daughter because soon she came in and she made me coffee and talked to me and was going back and forth from Marie to me. I think this went on for about three hours. Then the nurse called me in to the room and said, "It's all over now." I broke down and cried and cried.

I was guilty because I didn't help at the end. I didn't push myself to try hard enough. I told that to the nurse and she said, "Phil, you did great. You kept Marie alive for weeks longer than we thought possible." Boy, that made me feel good. I say those words to myself now when I get down.

Phil benefited from writing this account because the nurse's praise was there in front of him and he could read it whenever he needed to.

Artistic self-expression often produces healing, and when language turns your expression into a coherent story, you gain more advantages. Rambling journal entries help and may offer insight, but writing a story about your thoughts and your feelings actually will reduce any negativity you hold and increase feelings of calmness. Writing heals.

• *Write a poem about your relationship with the deceased.* Express all your feelings. Throughout the ages poets have lamented their losses. When the terrorists attacked on September 11, 2001, the United States Poet Laureate, Billy Collins, said that he could not immediately write a poem because the occasion was "too stupendous," and the terrorists had done something "beyond language." Nevertheless, poems written during grief abound. John Milton, William Shakespeare, Emily Dickinson, and Alfred Lord Tennyson wrote them; and more modern poets such as Sharon Olds and Tess Gallagher continue that tradition. Poet Robert Frost gave hope to many when he wrote, "In three words I can sum up everything I've learned about life: it goes on."

Poet and writer Judith Arcana wrote, "My mother was twenty-nine when she died, and I was only thirteen months old. Over the years, I've done many things to bring her back into my life: telling my women's group all about her death; playing her—in costume—as a character in my theater group; putting up her photos in my office, writing about her, and asking my family for their memories of her. Such a traumatic loss is never over, though I may have stopped consciously grieving in the past few years, in my sixties. Most recently, I wrote 'Dead Young Mother.' Here are the first few lines":

> My mother died
> when I was just
> a baby. So
> I look for her
> with the sweet hope
> of an infant.
> I look inside the memories
> of her brothers,
> the photographs
> in her album,
> pasted down in
> careful little
> corners.

—©2008 Judith Arcana

• *Make a list of adjectives to describe all the fine aspects of your beloved.* Writing positive words helps you feel more positive.
• *Write a letter to your loved one telling him all the things you want him to know.* It's okay to be challenging or negative if you wish. Writing this letter is therapeutic; mailing it is not. Keep the letter and look at it again every few months. Note your progress. It is a relief to express your pent-up thoughts and feelings. When they are put on paper—or computer screen—they are no longer only in your mind and can no longer cause you pain.

• *Write a letter to yourself as if it were written by your loved one.* The subject of the letter could be advice for you about your journey through bereavement and about your daily activities. Looking at yourself through the perspective of your beloved helps you know your next step.

• *Write a second letter to yourself as if it were written by your loved one.* This time, the letter could be about your life together. Let it be a letter of memories and reminiscences. Cherish this. Place it with photos and important keepsakes.

• *Write a story.* Narratives are important ways to make sense out of a life—and a death. Structuring your feelings and organizing your thoughts will help you feel better. The writer Joan Didion did just that after surviving the deaths of both her daughter and her husband. Her memoir, *The Year of Magical Thinking*, became a Broadway play, as well as a best-selling book.

It has been proved that when people write about events that upset them, their lives get better and their health improves. In fact, the more negativity that is written, the better the writer feels. Several consecutive days of writing is enough to change your mood. There have been clinical trials that encouraged writing by some of the people and told others not to write and still others to attend psychotherapy. The writers did as well as those in therapy as far as changing their mood and levels of anxiety.

Other literary forms including books and plays also help their authors move through the dark days of bereavement. C. S. Lewis wrote *A Grief Observed* after the death of his wife, Joy, to cancer in 1960; it is an account of the suffering and grief he went through.

A workbook of writing projects for the bereaved is available at www .solaceafteradeath.com.

ART IS THERAPY

If you are interested in expressing yourself artistically, you are in good company. Some mourners do not speak in words but express their feelings in creative ways by painting, sculpting, writing poetry, writing songs, essays, plays, and more. You don't have to be an accomplished artist or poet. You simply need to sit down and express your feelings. Novices and professional artists alike find artistic expression during bereavement therapeutic.

Rembrandt painted in grief. His wife died at just thirty years old in 1642 and in his grief Rembrandt painted *The Night Watch.* It has become one of his most famous works and is in Rijksmuseum in Amsterdam.

Picasso, after the death of his close friend and fellow artist, Henri Matisse, produced works incorporating some of the painting techniques Matisse was known for.

After Claude Monet's wife, Camille, died, he painted a series of melancholy still lifes including *Still Life with Pheasants and Plovers, Sunset on the Seine,* and *Winter.* Additionally, he painted one final portrait of her, *Camille Monet on her Deathbed,* which he never sold. Upon his death, it was given to the Musée d'Orsay in France, where it remains.

Celine Dion wrote the song "Fly" after her niece Karine died from complications of cystic fibrosis. Eric Clapton wrote the award-winning song "Tears in Heaven" when his young son died from an accidental fall. When John Lennon was murdered, Paul McCartney wrote "Here Today" about their years together.

Renoir, the French Impressionist painter, said, "The pain passes, but the beauty remains." Whether you are an artist, an amateur artist, or an observer of art, permit art to comfort you in your bereavement.

My client, Trudy, said that after her brother died when they were both in their twenties, she found comfort in her young daughter's coloring books and crayons. There was nothing to think about. She simply picked up a crayon and colored within the lines. After a couple of weeks, Trudy bought herself a sketch pad and some watercolors. She had never painted and certainly didn't consider herself to be an artist. But she was comforted by the relaxation that painting provided, and the calmness that she felt when looking at the soothing colors and shapes she created. Trudy says her first sign of recovery from the middle stage of bereavement was when she enrolled in a beginner's art class at the local community college.

> 🌿 *Suggestions from Carol in Long Island*
>
> *My tip for you is music, music, music. When my dad died I was twenty-five. He was sick a long time with cancer, during which time I withdrew from him. I feel guilty about that, but my mother insisted we weren't allowed to talk about his sickness. My parents always said he was fine. We had to pretend everything was normal, which was awkward and uncomfortable for me. I stayed home and cried a lot, holding articles of his clothing. Music helped. Especially Bob Marley's "No Woman, No Cry," which helped very much. I still cry when I hear that song.* 🌿

LEARNING IS THERAPY

Positive self-esteem helps you to adjust to your new lifestyle, a lifestyle that includes an empty chair. The best way to increase self-esteem is to become good at doing something. There are adult, continuing education classes at your local high school, at your local college, and at the library, too. Locate a YMCA or JCC and other community resources. Learn a new skill.

There is a reciprocal relationship between competence and a good adjustment to the loss of a loved one. Take a one-day class or a full-term class. Attend a one-hour lecture or a summer school session. Learn how to do a magic trick or learn how to grow orchids. Learn, learn, learn.

Is there something that's always interested you? Now is the time to pursue that interest. Do you want to learn to juggle? Do you want to learn how to play mah-jongg? How about a course in beekeeping? Maybe you've always wanted to know more about politics and would like a class in current events. Maybe you've always wanted to know how to use your digital camera. You can take a photography course. Learn country dancing or learn to play the piano. Learn to become a real estate appraiser or learn to bake a cake. Learning becomes you.

READING IS THERAPY

At first, you may find it too difficult to concentrate on a lengthy book and you'd be wise to read only short pamphlets, magazine articles, and then selected chapters. There are a plethora of books about grief, about death, and about surviving loss. At the back of this book, in the Appendix, you will find a list of such books. I've chosen only those books that many of my clients have found helpful.

Please don't limit your reading to bereavement books. Reading can be your great escape to other lands and to other centuries. Novels may intrigue you and take your mind away from your sadness. Memoirs may engage you in someone else's life. Mysteries may compel you to use your brain to ponder a dilemma belonging to someone else, not you—a welcome relief.

SWEET MOMENTS

Pay attention to those times when you are feeling peaceful. What are you doing at those moments? Keep a written or a mental list of things you do that give you solace. If an unhappy moment pops up, just consult your list and you'll know just how to get back to your sweet moment.

Here is a compilation of lists from some of my clients who were asked to complete the phrase "I feel really good when I . . ."

- Chat with my sister on the phone.
- Take the dog for a long walk.
- Look at photos of our last vacation.
- Ride my exercise bike.
- Play online games.
- Listen to music.
- Take a bubble bath.
- Pray.
- Watch the sunrise.
- Listen to a comforting CD.
- Catch up on work-related reading.
- Watch some sitcoms.
- Go to the movies.

- Work on my scrapbook.
- Get a manicure.
- Visit the grandchildren.
- Clean and clean and clean—the garage, the basement, everything.
- Work overtime and look for more work projects.
- Take a long drive.
- Cuddle up with some of his clothes.
- Hang out with his friends. They remind me of him.
- Look at beautiful art at a museum or gallery.
- Visit a park; take a hike.

✑ *Suggestions from Jan in California*

I was fifty-three and Jack was sixty-three when he died. I wish I would have known someone around my age who had walked the path of grief in a way that was inspiring or that I could have learned from. I wish I would have known that we were woefully underinsured. I became completely incapacitated by grief. I cried buckets. I wailed so loudly my neighbors were worried. I drank too much for about a year, until I got sick of myself. I had to stop watching Animal Planet or any movie where people died because I would cry so easily.

If you are newly bereaved I strongly encourage you to pay attention to what comforts you and ask for it. One day it may be being alone and the next day it may be going out. If you don't pay attention and ask for what you need, others will want you to do what comforts them.

I found that allowing the waves of grief to come over me and not resisting them helped them pass quicker.

Let people at work know what they can do to support you. They don't mean to be clueless.

I am no longer suffering. Thank God. ✑

It's time for you to compose your own personal list.

You can make your own list right here. Turn to it when you are feeling out of sorts.

I feel really good when I do the following—

Outside of the house: _____

_____

_____

Inside my home: _____

_____

_____

By myself: _____

_____

_____

With others: _____

_____

_____

At night if I cannot sleep: _____

_____

_____

Additional sources of comfort: _____

CHAPTER 4

Help from Others

You are not alone. Help is available. You may decide to turn to your neighbor, your rabbi, your coach, or your counselor—or to your minister, your mother, your psychotherapist, or your librarian. Whomever you choose will have advice. Then it's up to you to decide whose advice you will follow. This chapter will get you started. It provides an overview of all the ways in which you can obtain bereavement help.

BEREAVEMENT GROUPS

The majority of adults who are widowed or lose a parent or other loved one need only the support of a friend or family member. Within a year or two, they are back to the way they were before the death, and they are able to get through their day without a problem. Most people are resilient; after a death they experience severe transitory distress and then get over it.

> ✍ *Suggestions from Betsy in Los Angeles*
>
> *I wish someone would have told me to talk more about my loss and what I was going through. I was polite and I didn't want to bore anyone so I came home from being with friends full of fears and tears. If I had talked to the*

women at lunch I would have been relieved, but I thought it was not good manners to bring up how bad I was feeling. Now I realize, how could they help me if I didn't let them know I was suffering? My advice is to speak up, even if it means you might cry or choke up. 🖎

Bereavement groups can sometimes be useful, though, even to those who will recover by themselves. If you always feel better when you are with like-minded people, a group will be useful to you. Or, if you are lonely and want companionship, this is a good way to begin social interactions. If you are not a talker and are not one to share your feelings, then you may not enjoy a tell-all support group but may benefit from a bereavement group conducted in a less intrusive manner. It's the personality of the leader of the group that usually determines whether or not the agenda includes baring your soul. Some leaders are low key and do not encourage the sharing of feelings unless you, the bereaved, initiate it. My advice is to go to a meeting and then decide if it meets your needs. You'll know if you are comfortable there, or not.

Mutual support helps because people going through similar experiences can offer advice to one another. They know what works and what does not work. They are on the front lines. During your bereavement, you may become ultra aware of all those people who are enjoying a relationship that you no longer have. If your spouse passed away, you see married couples wherever you are. If your parent passed away, it seems you are the only one without a mom or dad. If your child died, you may believe no one else has ever had such a catastrophic loss. But, thankfully, in your bereavement group everyone is just like you.

Members of your bereavement group serve as your role models. They are living proof that you can survive this trauma. They offer tangible evidence that life goes on. Only another person who has gone through what you are going through can offer you practical advice about day-to-day situations. There are vital bits of information best provided by members of your bereavement support group.

If you have become widowed and don't know many other widowed people, you'll benefit from talking to others who have recently lost a mate. Members of your widow's group will tell you if, why, and when they removed their wedding bands or perhaps moved their rings to their other hand. They will share tips about dealing with in-laws and dealing with that clothes closet. They know about Social Security and they know about sitting alone in a restaurant.

> 🌿 *Suggestions from Mary in New York City*
>
> *I wore my husband's ring on a chain around my neck for a year. I also never changed his pillowcase so that I could have his scent in bed with me. After a year, I put the ring in my jewelry case and I finally changed the bed linen. I recommend you have something close to you that reminds you of your loved one.* 🌿

Clients tell me that their support group members help them in ways I never could. If you have lost a child, you will benefit from meeting other parents in the same circumstance. Losing a child creates immeasurable grief and pain, no matter the age of that child. Grieving parents often feel that their friends become strangers, because those friends cannot understand the depths of their sorrow. When those grieving parents join a bereaved-parents support group, they feel that the strangers in the group become friends. Those are the people who can understand; they have been there. They know about removing cribs from the nursery and removing toys from the toy closet. They know about the sensitive handling of siblings and of grandparents, too.

> 🌿 *Suggestions from a Father of Three in Philadelphia*
>
> *My tip to you if you suffered the tragedy of losing a child is to make an agreement with your spouse and your children as to what you will say to people when they ask how many are in your family. My daughters were perplexed when schoolmates asked if they had a brother. They used to have one and they didn't know what to say. My wife and I didn't either. When people would ask how many kids we had, we felt disloyal by leaving out Freddy. Sometimes telling someone would make them so sad that I wound up comforting them. Once, to cheer up someone who got so upset when she heard about Freddy's passing, I told her that she shouldn't feel so bad, it was okay. Believe me, it's never going to be okay.* 🌿

Parents who have lost a child are particularly grateful to other parents who help them to once again relate to the outside world—the world beyond severe grief. For example, the answer to the question that bereaved parents dread—"How many children do you have?"—is regularly discussed at bereaved-parent meetings. Parents report that at the beginning of bereavement if a well-meaning acquaintance should ask that question it can set off hysterics or, as Betty recounted, "I just ran away, jumped into my car, and headed for home and bed." Parents need each other and learn from one another.

In *Recovering from the Loss of a Child,* Katherine Fair Donnelly writes, "Parents want to talk. They need someone to listen to the crying of their soul." Donnelly adds, "The shock impact of a child's death leaves parents with one of the cruelest of all emotions—the total sense of powerlessness." Parents assume they can protect their child. Those parents whose child has died are forced to acknowledge that they are not in control and their child has succumbed even though they tried their best.

Disenfranchised Grief

You would do well to join a bereavement group if your loss cannot be openly acknowledged or publicly announced. The term for this type of grief is *disenfranchised grief.*

A member of a bereavement group for parents whose children died of a drug overdose told me she felt guilty for feeling relieved after her son's death. "I was always waiting for that horrendous call from the police. After Karl died, I could sleep through the night and not be worried. I thought I must be a terrible mother for feeling that way but every other parent in the group understood and no one blamed me."

Another member of that group said, "I used to wish Gina passed away from something more honorable, like cancer or a car accident, instead of from an overdose. Those parents in my bereavement group set me straight and I owe them all a debt of gratitude."

My friend Julie needed the support of a group when her ex-husband died. Richard had been out of her life for decades. Julie was happily remarried. When Richard died, though, Julie felt bereft. She wanted to talk about the innocence with which they met and married. She wanted to reminisce about their dreams and hopes when they had their babies. Well, her husband didn't want to hear it—it was hurtful to him. Her adult children were dealing with their grief for their father in their own way and it did not include their mother, but rather their stepmother. Julie went to a bereavement group, cried her tears, spoke her mind, and after a couple of months gained enough strength to resign from the group. It had served an excellent purpose.

Caroline and Lana were sisters for whom the term *sibling rivalry* must have been created. They envied each other, sabotaged each other, and constantly bickered. When they were children, their parents thought they'd outgrow their competitiveness when each would have her own apartment. During young adulthood, their respective husbands thought they'd outgrow it when each would have her own children. To everyone's dismay Caroline and Lana fought with each other whenever they got together, which was quite often. Even after children, even after grandchildren, they were still at it. Lana showed up at my office soon after Caroline died from a surgical procedure gone awry. Lana said she needed a bereavement counselor because everyone who knew her thought she'd be relieved and no one understood that she was mourning. She wanted the opportunity to express all her feelings without being told, "You never liked your sister. Stop crying."

You have disenfranchised grief if you lost someone under the following conditions:

- Lost your secret lover
- Lost your ex-spouse whom you still loved
- Lost your pet who was like a child to you
- Lost a family member who was a suicide
- Lost a family member who was murdered
- Lost a family member who died from a drug overdose
- Lost someone with whom you had a difficult and stormy relationship
- Lost someone who had AIDS

These situations, and some others, typically can exclude you from receiving the social support you need. It is important for your recovery that you speak about your situation, and fortunately these are circumstances easily spoken about within the confines of a bereavement group.

Suicide is not always acknowledged. Some people still attach shame or stigma to a suicide and do not understand that suicide is usually the result of a disease—a brain gone awry. Fortunately, there are signs that the stigma is gradually being lifted. At the recent funeral of a middle-age woman who had killed herself, the priest said, "The suicide is a puzzle. Each mourner in this room has one piece of that puzzle. God, though, has the final piece. So now our beloved is whole again." A Catholic burial for a woman who killed herself was once unheard of.

CARMELLA'S STORY

I felt like an idiot because no one else in my family even cared that our father died, but I was crying and crying. He was a mean man and was cruel to us when we were growing up. My mother divorced him and remarried a very sweet guy whom we all called Dad. We would see my father at Christmas for a few minutes and that was it.

When the police called to say he was dead in his apartment, my brother called me and I called my two sisters. We all went to pay our respects at the funeral home. No one else was there. The old man had alienated everyone who ever tried to be nice to him.

But I felt too sad to run out and leave after a short time, the way my brother and sisters did. I wanted to stay and hang out with my father. I wanted to talk to him and ask him why he didn't like us. I wanted to tell him that if he ever was just a little bit interested in me, I would have been very interested in him. If he tried for a minute, I would try for an hour just because I wanted a real father. But all I could do was stand next to the casket and sob.

For the next few months, I thought about him all the time. I imagined him as a good guy and not as he really was. When I made myself remember his meanness, I cried even more. When he died, I think I cried for all the times when he was alive and I should have cried but held it in. I finally stopped carrying on about him when I realized that he stopped being my father years ago and his death did not change anything. I went to visit my mom and step-father and for the first time in my life, I bought a present for my stepfather.

LINDA'S STORY

My husband died at age 55, I was 57. It was a traumatic death because it was witnessed by me and my children.

When the EMS workers were in the house, they did not tell me that my husband was already clinically dead. So I still had hope.

When we got to the hospital, the ER staff just told me he was "very sick." These euphemisms made the actual pronouncement much more shocking for all of us.

There was no counselor at the hospital. The three of us just had to go home on our own. We had come in an ambulance so we didn't have our car. It was an unbelievable event for us. I know that for rape victims the hospital provides a rape counselor and they also drive the victim home after the hospital visit. Why not do the same for a family that just had a death? We were left on our own.

Afterward, there was no contact made by the hospital to give us a bereavement group. I later found one on my own that coinciden-tally is connected to the exact same hospital. It seems that unless the patients' families seek it out, they would never know there is some-thing available.

My suffering now is not only for myself. My kids lost their dad and that is as hard for me to cope with as is my personal loss as a wife who lost her beloved husband.

Group Benefits

You may find that your group gives you the opportunity to talk about your beloved in a way that brings him or her back to life for you during the meetings. This helps you more easily confront the reality of your loss. After a while, at your own pace, you will allow the image of your beloved to become a comforting memory. Within your group you can remember the good times, and the bad, go over the details of the death, and then use the group members' input to plan your future.

A bereavement group gives you the forum in which to discuss subjects your friends and family may not be interested in. Like you, others who are bereaved wonder about the unfairness of life.

- Do you get upset when you see strangers walking in the street who are older than your beloved?
- Do you get upset when you see people of poor character who are still alive?

The randomness of disease is most apparent when you visit a hospital and see severe suffering, and then visit a prison where many inmates are in perfect health and will live out their full lifespan. Life can be unjust. We do not necessarily get what we deserve. Sometimes the good do die young. Sometimes calamities strike randomly. Your group members well understand this.

In a good bereavement group, you are free to express feelings without fear of criticism. Friends and family, on the other hand, want you to quickly race through bereavement and return to your old self. Because they mean well and it pains them to see you so sad, they tend to offer unsolicited advice and urge a rapid recovery. They just don't get it—you will recover, but at your own pace. This has been a known fact forever. The Old Testament contains a passage that is helpful and wise in times of grief, no matter your religion or lack thereof:

> To every thing there is a season,
> And a time to every purpose under the heaven:
> A time to be born, and a time to die;
> A time to plant, and a time to pluck up that which is planted;
> A time to kill, and a time to heal;
> A time to break down, and a time to build up;
> A time to weep, and a time to laugh;
> A time to mourn, and a time to dance;

A time to cast away stones, and a time to gather stones together;
A time to embrace, and a time to refrain from embracing;
A time to get, and a time to lose;
A time to keep, and a time to cast away;
A time to rend, and a time to sew;
A time to keep silence, and a time to speak;
A time to love, and a time to hate;
A time of war, and a time of peace.
—ECCLESIASTES 3:1–8

Bereavement groups have been valuable for centuries. Beginning in the twelfth century, Jewish mourners have recited a traditional prayer called the *Kaddish*. From the day of burial, continuing for eleven months after the death of a parent, religious Jewish mourners gather with other members of their synagogue once, or even twice, each day, to chant the prescribed words. This may seem burdensome, but the practice of saying Kaddish is effective for the following reasons:

• *Grief reactions are normalized.* When others in your group are going through precisely what you are going through, you tend to feel that your reactions and responses are exactly right.
• *Emotional expression is encouraged.* You are supposed to chant the words with feeling, and they are particularly powerful words. It is a passionate recitation.
• *Faith is promoted.* The prayer itself is a public praise to God uttered at just the time when a life has been taken and faith may be faltering.
• *Quiet support is offered.* Everyone in the congregation knows you are there to mourn a loved one and is respectful of your situation. There is a specific time during the religious service that mourners are asked to stand and say Kaddish.

Saying Kaddish drags a person out of the house and interrupts the person's isolation at a time when he or she may be tempted to stay under the covers for days at a time. This custom provides structure in a day that could easily become disorganized and disordered. The first mourners to say Kaddish may have inadvertently established the world's first bereavement support group.

The best part of a support group is that giving help is the best way to get help. When someone more recently bereaved than you enters your group you will, for a moment, leave your dependent state and uncover your strengths. That is a good thing for you and for the new group member.

BEREAVEMENT COUNSELORS—PROS AND CONS

Sensitive psychological support is always warranted during bereavement, but grief-focused therapy is needed only for the few mourners who develop complicated grief. Complicated grief, as discussed earlier, is extreme and excessive mourning that does not let up.

Usually, if bereavement therapy is needed at all, it would be an appropriate intervention several months after the death, not immediately after.

Sometimes counselors insist that you need their services if a loved one has died. A bereavement counselor may wish to meet with you to help you make your way through the bereavement process. Trust me, you know how to grieve—you don't need a teacher. Normal reactions need not be analyzed.

If bereavement counseling is to be useful, it is best offered at several months to a year after the death. That's the time when mourners know if they still have issues about the death. And certainly that's when mourners know if they have complicated grief. Most people, though, will be feeling fine by then. Please consult a bereavement counselor if you have come down with a case of complicated grief.

I do not recommend bereavement counseling immediately after a death. When well-meaning counselors rush to a school after a student's death or hasten to the scene of a shooting, they may do more harm than good. For many people, talking about the death immediately after it occurs interrupts that natural numbness cycle that is meant to be protective. Such talk may increase sadness. It's better to permit the sadness to follow its natural pace and gradually emerge and then gradually dissipate.

High school teacher Nancy Rehm says, "When our small rural school experienced an epidemic of suicides, we were descended upon by outside experts. What we learned was that it is absolutely emotionally intolerable to be around anyone who had not known the student. Outsiders should say nothing more than, 'I'm sorry.' "

In New York City, after September 11, mental-health professionals thought they would be bombarded with clients seeking counseling. Instead, there was no great influx of people clamoring for appointments. Symptoms of extreme stress diminish with time. Most mourners get better on their own.

Sometimes it's better to use common sense than to listen to professionals. Yes, there may be a time in your journey through bereavement when you will wish to speak to a professional. But until the time when you, yourself, feel the need to initiate that conversation, it is unwise to dwell on certain memories and it is unwise to talk about situations that will make you feel worse.

You may wish to consult a professional counselor to help you figure out some next steps to take. It's usually a good idea to proceed with caution. Don't make any drastic changes in your life immediately after a death.

🌿 Suggestions from Mike in Ohio

My minister told me not to make any changes for at least one year. But I didn't listen and thought I knew better. I sold my house and now I not only miss my wife, I miss my house. My advice is don't make any major changes for the first year. 🌿

TERRY'S STORY

At our wedding, Sal quoted Robert Browning, "Grow old with me, the best is yet to be." We didn't know that he would never grow beyond age 45. I was thirty-eight and my world as I knew it ended that day when cancer got the best of him. We had been together for eighteen years. I was the first of my friends and family to experience the death of a spouse. Even my parents were still married.

My grief was overwhelming. It controlled me and consumed me. It ripped through me like a knife and left me with an open wound. It was as if a scab grew over the wound, but if I turned the wrong way the scab would reopen. The grief kept reappearing and reopening the wound. I don't think I ever got over it, but I have learned to adapt to life without my husband. The pain is eased but not entirely gone.

When I finally dragged myself to a therapist, he had no clue what to do with me. He told me to go to a happy hour and find new friends. I should have stopped after my second appointment but I continued for a while longer.

Eventually, I found a therapist who was experienced with grief. She helped me. She also guided me to do volunteer work with widows. I went back to school for a master's degree in grief counseling. I'm planning my future and now I have dreams.

Repression

Repression is a process your mind uses unconsciously, without your help, without your permission, and without your knowledge. It happens by itself. Repression keeps painful memories and thoughts out of your mind. Repression helps your recovery. In cases of serious loss and trauma, such as death by fire or car accident or violence, your mind's ability to use repression to prevent memories from coming up is a blessing.

Do not be misled by overeager bereavement counselors who are guided by outdated information. We used to think, erroneously, that psychological havoc would result if you did not experience intense emotions. Grief counselors insisted that clients express deep emotions and goaded clients into finding such hidden feelings. Today, we know better. Repression is not pathological and you will have your best outcome if you make the decision about if and when to speak to a counselor.

Of course, you know that you do need bereavement counseling if your grief response is so severe that you cannot get back into relationships, into work, into life. If people you live with or work with suggest that you should have a consultation with a grief specialist, please do so. Usually just a few sessions will do the trick. Or, medication may be recommended and that will help you.

The Myth of Closure

Closure is a myth. Don't think you need a bereavement counselor if you have not finished thinking about your loved one. Paul, a friend, explains:

> "My brother has been dead for eighteen years, and the thing that amazes me the most is that he just pops up. A word, a phrase, or I could be playing golf or just standing by the grill, and out of nowhere there is a vivid memory of him. I actually feel him next to me. Often, I immediately smile, but later I may be a little sad."

You will probably enjoy reminiscing and remembering for the rest of your life. Please remember the good times. Most people continue their emotional relationship with the deceased even though the physical relationship has ended. You can go on to love again and still maintain your love for the deceased. You don't have to forget.

Did you know that some widowers never stop crying until the day they remarry?

Do not be misled by therapists or clergy who want you to find meaning in the death. Many times it is impossible to make sense out of an untimely or violent death. Some deaths are meaningless. They are random acts of unfairness, violence, or more. Don't waste your energy hunting around for a hidden meaning.

Richard Attenborough, the English actor, director, and producer, lost his daughter and granddaughter, who were vacationing in Thailand, in the tsunami of 2004. Several years later, Attenborough wrote about the way in which he and his wife have coped:

> If I stop and think about it, I just cry. It was the most terrible day of our lives. . . . We have . . . an ability to compartmentalize grief

and put it in a place we can revisit when we choose. . . . . There is joy to recall, too. . . . . You just have to reach down into your memory to find it.

Help for Military Widows

Military widows usually benefit from bereavement counseling. If your spouse was killed in the military, you are probably younger than most widows and you may have small children. It's likely that you are living away from your extended family. All these circumstances can make it more difficult for you to cope, and you will benefit from joining a bereavement support group or seeing a counselor or psychotherapist for individual therapy.

Military widows often report that emphasis is placed on their spouse's heroism and sacrifice. Sometimes people feel that you must be so proud of your spouse that you will soon bounce back from this horrendous trauma. No one is informing you that the bereavement process may take years. In fact, most of the military widows and widowers with whom I've worked have had to educate their parents, who consistently told them to start dating and stop mourning. That is not good advice. Thus, military widows need a place where they can vent their feelings about:

- Their parents' inability to help them
- Their sudden change of status and identity
- Their children's dependency
- Their children's acting out
- Their attempts to date others on the base
- The unfairness of life

Young military widows, if isolated and uninformed, run the risk of depression. If you are the spouse of someone who was killed while serving the country, please get evaluated for depression so that if you do come down with a case of depression it can be treated before it escalates.

YOUR FUNERAL DIRECTOR

Your funeral director, formerly called an undertaker or mortician, can be useful to you. Significant support and guidance for the family of the deceased may be available at your local funeral home. Funeral directors have plenty of experience in dealing with folks in your situation and many directors also have special training in bereavement counseling. In polls, mourners, particularly parents who have lost a child, often report that it was their funeral director who offered the most help in their time of need.

In many towns, cities, and suburbs, too, there are local, family-owned funeral homes that have cared for every deceased member of generations of a family. That tradition is always a comfort to the family. It is that sign of familiarity, a known ritual during a time of chaos, that helps the family members. The care is personal, all actions are respectful, and simply speaking to the funeral director is a comfort to the survivors.

Carl Goldman, director of a memorial chapel in Massachusetts, explains that in recent years psychologically oriented programs have been established in many funeral homes. He says that whether the owner is a local family or part of a large chain, you, the consumer, need not worry. As long as there is a stable management team in place, your bereavement needs will be met. For example, the Dignity Memorial Company has produced excellent brochures as one component of its Pick Up the Pieces Program, and those brochures are available free of charge at Dignity-affiliated funeral homes.

Your funeral director will know your next step and will also know what your particular religion offers you. When in doubt, follow your religion's policies and systems; after all, they've helped others of your faith for centuries.

Interestingly, it is funeral directors who coined the term, *living room*, for that somewhat formal room in your home that contains the sofa and chairs. Traditionally, dead people were laid out in a room called the parlor, and visitors came to the family's home to pay their respects. Funeral directors wanted to do more than just bury the dead. They wanted to hold services in their facility and they started a campaign to move the dead people out of the family's parlor into the funeral home. "How lovely your home will be," they said, "if that room did not hold the deceased, but was, instead, a room of life, a living room."

There was a time when funeral directors were considered harbingers of death and even their closest friends and their family members were reluctant to invite them to social events for fear of offending other guests. Funeral directors are no longer shunned. In fact, from 2001 to 2005 the popular TV show *Six Feet Under*, about a family and their family business—a funeral home—captivated America's attention. The show won three Golden Globe Awards, nine Emmy Awards, and one Peabody Award.

YOUR FAMILY AND FRIENDS

Family members tend to rise to the occasion. When a death hits one part of the family, it is often the extended family—cousins, aunts, uncles, nieces, nephews, even ex-spouses and ex-in-laws—who will lend a hand and lend an ear. Don't permit petty rivalries, jealousies, or long-ago estrangements to get in the way of connecting to blood relatives. Blood counts, especially at the time of a death.

🌿 Suggestions from Sally in Texas

Don't move in with your kids. I thought I wouldn't be able to live alone and I gave up my apartment. What a mistake that was. I should have just lived with my daughter for the first few months when the grief was fresh because now I could definitely be on my own. But it's too late. I can't get to my friends or my doctor or my dentist or my beauty parlor. Everything is new here and it's a very big adjustment. Don't move in with your kids. 🌿

🌿 *Suggestions from David in Phoenix*

After a few months I knew it was time to clear out my wife's clothes. Every time I went to her closet I got too choked up and couldn't do it. So I asked my neighbor to help. She's a nice lady and she had asked if she could do something for me after Jill died. Well, my daughters still haven't spoken to me. They are furious that I had a stranger and not them go through their mother's clothes. I thought I was sparing the girls from the anguish of going through their mother's garments. It practically destroyed me when I started to work on the closet. But I should have asked them and not the neighbor. I was wrong. My advice to you is ask your children to help you before you ask anyone else. 🌿

Neighbors may merely nod or barely smile, but they know you and they know your daily habits. Your neighbors are aware that you have suffered a loss and they probably want to do something to help you. They may not realize that all you'd like from them is ten minutes of conversation or a ride to a store. Figure out which neighbors and which friends you can count on for which purposes. This is the time when it is perfectly okay to use people. You are using their good will to help yourself function. They benefit because it's a joy to help someone and know that you are making them feel better, while you benefit because it's a relief to know there is someone nearby on whom you can rely. Don't think you must entertain the folks from down the street. All you need to do is say "thank you" when they appear with food or with advice.

🌿 *Suggestions from M.N., a Widower in Colorado*

Sharon loved to read. When our neighbors wanted to do something, all I could think of was telling them to pray. I should have asked them to donate a book in her name to the town library. Maybe the library would have set up a shelf called Sharon's Shelf for all the donated books. But now it's too late for me. It's not too late for you. 🌿

> 🌿 *Suggestions from John in New York*
>
> *My advice is call people you want to talk to. I felt alone after my daughter passed away and a year later I found out that many people were concerned about me but were too shy or awkward to make the first move. Death intimidates people. Especially the death of a child.* 🌿

> 🌿 *Suggestions from Bobbi in Florida*
>
> *I would have done better if I had something prepared to say when people asked what they could do to help. I should have said that they could drive me places because I often felt too shaky to drive. My advice is know what you want other people to do for you and then when they ask you can make your request.* 🌿

> 🌿 *Suggestions from Stephanie in Wisconsin*
>
> *My advice is to call your old friends. People from the past care about you because of your shared history. They were all helpful to me. None of my present-day friends really knew my mother but my old friends knew her well from when we were young. It's still good to talk to them now.* 🌿

The Unhelpful

Sometimes you'll encounter people who are well intentioned—they may actually love you—yet they do the wrong thing or say the wrong words. They want to be helpful. They try to be helpful. But, they fail at helping. Often, in fact, they unintentionally make you feel worse. They may so much want you to recover from bereavement that they practically drag you out into the harsh realities of the world when you still need to be in your cocoon of safety.

Many of my clients tell me they get furious at well-meaning friends and family who unknowingly say hurtful comments. When Carol's baby died of

SIDS a neighbor, hoping to help Carol, said, "At least the baby was very young and you didn't get to know him or love him as much as you love your older children. That will make it easier to get over this." Carol was horrified and hurt. A baby, even a stillborn infant, is loved and is a repository of dreams and future plans.

Some well-meaning folks might implore you to get on with your life. They have no clue that simply leaving your bed and taking a shower is a major step. Ignore the comments from people who have never experienced what you are experiencing. They simply don't know. They don't understand that death is nonnegotiable. There is no way to make things right. Not now.

🌿 *Suggestions from Sarah in Vermont*

Tell people who bother you about your grieving that some days just getting dressed is a mighty effort and answering your mail is plenty difficult and they should not ask you to do anything more. It took me seven months to function the way others wanted me to and that was three years ago. In the last two years, I got raises at work and did many outstanding things. I wish I had told people to have more patience with me. 🌿

Then there are the people who will tell you about a person they know who suffered the same loss as you. These helpers will insist that if you do just what that person did, you will suddenly feel better. So they tell you about someone who went on a cruise and immediately stopped weeping, or someone who went back to school and became a genius, or someone else who bought a lottery ticket and won millions. Please remember, you are under no obligation to take advice from everyone who offers it.

FINANCIAL ASSISTANTS

You will need to take care of money, even if you never before did so. It is necessary for you to contact the human resources department of every company that your loved one ever worked for. They will know about pensions, 401(k)s, life insurance, and other employer-related benefits.

Also, call or go to your local Social Security office to find out what benefits you and other family members might be entitled to. Then, watch your mail for statements from banks and stock brokerages. That's how you will know what assets you must be concerned about and what bills you must pay.

When people ask how they can be useful to you at this time, mention that you would like to interview a financial planner or estate lawyer or anyone they know who is a finance professional. Please don't take financial advice from your neighbor, your niece, or your yoga instructor who moonlights as a tax-preparer.

🌿 *Suggestions from Gail in Maryland*

Hire an accountant if you have money issues to deal with. I tried to do it myself and then I asked my sister-in-law and then I asked my nephew. All that did for me was cause more stress. When I finally hired an accountant the stress was over. I wrote one check to him and that was that. He took care of everything. 🌿

🌿 *Suggestions from Eddie in Long Island*

My advice is don't tell everyone if you get a big life insurance payment. I did and four people wanted loans and then I took a group out on vacation and now I am still bereaved and I am broke. 🌿

FINDING HELP ON THE INTERNET

In the twenty-first century, it is appropriate to use your computer to find help. The Internet has many excellent resources for you to use during your bereavement.

Thanatos is the mythological Greek God of death. *Thanatology* is the study of death, dying, and bereavement. A *thanatologist* is a person who has advanced degrees in the study of death, the process of dying, and the cultural and religious theories surrounding death.

According to thanatologist Terry Oliveri:

Clients who use online support groups no longer have to schedule an appointment or attend a group session at a set time requiring re-arrangement of work, family, and social schedules. They can now send messages to their counselors or support groups at any time—night or day. The need to find comfort and support may occur at any time.

Online grief support groups work in the following way: Each grief support group has its own e-mail address; one member of the online grief support group sends an e-mail message to the group. Everyone in the group receives a copy of the message and anyone can respond to the message.

Oliveri interviewed members of an online bereavement support group and noted that their reasons for choosing an online, rather than a face-to-face, group were:

- Discomfort talking with family and friends
- Greater feeling of empathy among persons using online grief sup-port than with friends or family
- Convenience of use—92 percent of respondents stated the availabil-ity of receiving support at any time of day or night was significant
- Anonymity offered by online grief support groups

Ironically, Oliveri's personal experience with an online group was not all that positive. She joined a grief chat room after she was widowed and had the following experience:

I introduced myself and let myself remember those first months of being widowed. I typed in my mantra, the question that I asked my-self for months, and maybe even a year or two. "I'm thirty-eight and my husband died. My life is over. How do I go on with life and find a new life if I cannot remember what life was like before I met my husband?"

I felt by typing these words I was bearing my soul to the world. As I wrote these words, I remembered repeating them over and over when I was newly widowed and the emotions and feelings all came back. I felt as if I was standing naked.

The response I received from the host was: "We all go through that when we become widowed, honey."

I do not know which upset me more, this condescending statement or being called honey. I could not respond to it. I was greeted by the members who just came on and I watched the screen while they had conversations about cookies. I bared my soul and no one cared.

Additional investigation by Oliveri indicated the chat room host was not a counselor and the website had no professionals listed on its staff. If you decide to use the Internet, it's a good idea to carefully check all sites.

Websites

Here are bereavement sites that are professionally run and have proved useful to many of my clients:

Association of Death Education and Counseling (www.adec.org)

The Association of Death Education and Counseling (ADEC) educates professionals with various educational backgrounds—theologians, physicians, hospice workers, and others—about all aspects of death and bereavement.

The resources on this website are amazing. There are literally hundreds of links to websites ranging from an NPR show exploring death to a pet loss forum to a directory of Web cemeteries to a listing of Chinese grief websites, and on and on.

ADEC publishes a newsletter and several journals and also offers a certification procedure for thanatologists. There is an annual conference presenting scholarly papers whose scope reaches from a professor's theory about how children understand grief to a social scientist talking about the death system of Taiwan or to a physician explaining how to apply Buddhist psychology to grief counseling.

The design of this easy-to-navigate website is quite appealing. All the requisite information has been intelligently segregated into menu items. Information about every activity undertaken by ADEC is quickly accessible.

AARP (www.aarp.org/families/grief_loss or www.AARP/griefandloss)
All the practical information you need during bereavement is here. There are links to local support networks, to Social Security information, and to publications about bereavement. There are facts about psychological aspects of grief. There is specific financial help for widows, and you'll also find memorial ideas, and more.

The Childhood Bereavement Network
(www.childhoodbereavementnetwork.org.uk/)
The Childhood Bereavement Network (CBN) has an exceptional site for both parents and teachers. Nowadays, when a child is deathly ill, the parents do not hide that child at home, but rather find ways for the child to continue at school and participate in friendships. Thankfully, today death is spoken about in schools and the entire school may be called on to mourn the death of a student. This means that children are much more aware of and involved in death matters than the sheltered children of a previous generation.

The Childhood Bereavement Project was launched in 1998 and later supported by funds from the late Diana, Princess of Wales, Memorial Fund. The Childhood Bereavement Network operates under the umbrella of the National Children's Bureau and is a national charitable organization in the United Kingdom. The organization works closely with the British Parliament to develop national policies and guidelines to support bereaved children and young people. One of their projects, funded by the late Princess Diana, is Grief Matters for Children. Its aim is to raise awareness of bereaved children and then emotionally support them. The work by the CBN has also led to several legislative acts that have been passed in the Parliament. It is now acknowledged in the United Kingdom that bereavement in a child is a continuous learning process and that these children should be regularly followed, monitored, and evaluated.

The grand vision of this charitable organization is to ensure that all children with their families and health care providers in the United Kingdom have access to both local and international data to guide them through the process of bereavement. This organization has a network of members located throught the United Kingdom and they cater to the needs of all children.

There are tips for parents and teachers as well as tips for the children themselves. There are also videos available for sale to help older children with bereavement and jigsaw puzzles and postcards for the younger ones.

Lecacy.com (www.legacy.com)
Founded in 1998, Legacy.com provides an easy way to create an obituary that can then be placed in any newspaper. Legacy.com actually hosts the online obituary sites of leading newspapers and contributes obituary notices to more than

350 U.S. newspapers. The site attempts to provide community-oriented information about the deceased and therefore augments obituaries with guest books, funeral home information, florist links, and other useful information. Backed by several investors, the chief motive of Legacy.com is to provide innovative ways to celebrate people's lives.

In addition to the existing obituary resources, Legacy.com offers an online support community. Membership is free and discussion boards include a variety of topics, from dealing with a sudden loss to helping a bereaved loved one. A member can post pictures.

You are encouraged to create a tribute to your beloved and that tribute will remain online. You are invited to add music, text, photos, and even your own voice to the website.

Legacy.com offers articles written by professionals on how to deal with grief and also offers professionally written poetry. This website has new inspirational articles posted every day. The site has an online gift shop from which you can send tasteful floral arrangements, comforting care baskets, and other encouraging items.

The Compassionate Friends (www.compassionatefriends.org)
According to the founder of this organization, "The Compassionate Friends is about transforming the pain of grief into the elixir of hope. It takes people out of the isolation society imposes on the bereaved and lets them express their grief naturally. With the shedding of tears, healing comes. And the newly bereaved get to see people who have survived and are learning to live and love again."

Each year 150,000 children and young adults die in the United States—and these statistics do not include miscarriages, stillbirths, or the deaths of adult children over age 40. The Compassionate Friends (TCF) is for the parents, grandparents, and siblings of those deceased children.

In addition to offering the latest news and resources on grief management, the website teaches family members how to support one another and also gives them the opportunity to form communities of like-minded people with whom to share their bereavement. Veteran grievers become role models to the newly bereaved and in doing so they, too, benefit.

There are online groups and local chapters. There are regional and national TCF conferences and an annual Walk to Remember. One of the educational goals of the group is to end the myth that the divorce rate is unusually high after a child's death. Statistics do not bear out this false information and TCF is adamant that it is harmful to the newly bereaved couple to continue to hear that their marriage is doomed.

Grief Net (www.griefnet.org)

Set up by Cendra Lynn, psychologist and traumatologist, GriefNet.org is an Internet community of people coping with sorrow, death, and loss. It provides a large forum for sharing feelings.

GriefNet runs more than fifty e-mail support groups, and provides the opportunity to create a memorial for the deceased. Resources offered include a library of both factual and inspirational articles, poems, and information and ideas related to death, bereavement, and suicide prevention. An annotated bibliography offers books and music via Amazon. GriefNet.org is a safe haven during bereavement.

Additionally, GriefNet provides kidsaid.com. This is a remarkable part of GriefNet.org that gives a bereaved child every possible comfort as well as information. This site also offers access to online and in-person counseling. Arrangements can be made for reduced rates or payment plans if needed.

The Sibling Connection (www.counselingstlouis.net)

The Sibling Connection is a not-for-profit organization based in St. Louis, Missouri. The organization offers this website for individuals grieving the loss of a sibling. The site offers age-specific articles on how to deal with the grief of losing a brother or a sister. It also has articles on supporting parents after a sibling's death and it includes book and movie lists to help siblings deal with their own grief. Especially striking are the movie reviews that discuss the impact each film would have on a grieving person.

The Valley of Life (www.valleyoflife.com)

This is a site for memorialization and remembrance. Begun by a woman who wanted to memorialize her mother, this site takes you through the steps of creating a Web page for your loved one. You can add photos, music, videos, and more. This is all free. You can have a guest book, and friends and family can record their memories here, too. You can build a family tree. You can blog and share your thoughts, feelings, and ideas with everyone who visits this site. Personal stories may be posted here, too. There is a discussion board and there is a gift shop that sells floral arrangements and gift baskets.

Hospice Net (www.hospicenet.org/html/bereavement.html)

Hospice Net is an excellent site that provides practical information and support to patients and families who are faced with life-threatening medical disorders. The website has detailed knowledge about the role of caregivers and their journey through hospice. Bereavement is fully discussed and a step-by-step approach to managing grief is presented. The readings are simple and easy to understand.

The Grief Recovery Institute (www.grief.net)

Under the heading "Helpful Articles," you can access nearly one hundred articles written by the Institute's founders: John W. James and Russell Friedman. The articles can be downloaded and printed at no cost. You will find information and schedules for the Grief Recovery Personal Workshops and there is detailed information about Grief Recovery Certification Training Programs. (Be aware that while you might obtain a good education about grief, a grief certification program is not recognized by any local, state, or federal institution or organization.)

Society of Military Widows (www.militarywidows.org)

The Society of Military Widows was established nearly forty years ago by Theresa Alexander. This nonprofit organization was developed to serve the families of men who had died while on active military duty. Initially, the organization offered only emotional support but over the years has developed a national reputation as a champion for benefits for the widows, widowers, and children of deceased military personnel. The organization offers a variety of social support services including grief counseling and general assistance. It does not provide online services but offers support services from individuals who may be living near you. If there is an emergency, the site does provide ample resources for help. The society does not have professional counselors working for it but does have referral sources.

The National Organization of Parents of Murdered Children (www.pomc.com)

Despite its name, the National Organization of Parents of Murdered Children (POMC) is actually a resource for *any* person who is grieving the loss of a murdered person no matter the relationship. POMC is not just a support group; it is also an advocacy group that aids families' fight for justice in the criminal justice system. POMC also provides training to social workers and attorneys who want to help after a murder.

The American Widow Project (www.Americanwidowproject.org)

The American Widow Project is a nonprofit organization for widows of men who were killed while on duty in the military. The project's emphasis is on healing through sharing stories, tears, and laughter. There is also a hotline that is available twenty-four hours a day, seven days a week. No counselors are on the hotline. Instead, you will be speaking to another widow who has dealt with your situation. You also can be provided with the phone number of a military widow in or close to your neighborhood.

The American Widow Project has a networking system that will connect you to individuals in your community who will volunteer their time and services, whether it be babysitting or counseling, to show their thanks and appreciation for the sacrifice your family has made. This site has widows' stories and hints and much more. It is a splendid resource.

RD4U (www.rd4u.org.uk)

RD4U, short for "the road for you," is a website funded by the Children's Bereavement Network. It was created by young people, ages 16 to 25, to help other children and young adults around the world grieve for the loss of a loved one.

The website has short, easy-to-read articles on grief and bereavement, suitable for kids. Each article has suggestions for coping activities or pain management tailored specifically for children. Younger bereaved children will enjoy using the balloon messages and memory boxes.

There is a fun zone, a gallery where children can post pictures and drawings, and a message board where children can talk to one another. Interestingly, there is a message board reserved just for boys. The site designers created this to facilitate emotional sharing among boys, who are usually not as quick to expose their feelings as are girls.

Grief's Journey (www.GriefsJourney.com)

Grief's Journey is a site dedicated to those who have lost a spouse or partner. It is a comprehensive community with links to many helpful articles. You will also find personal poetry and essays written by widows and widowers.

Grief's Journey has a media section that includes movie clips and reviews chosen specifically for their content relating to widowhood. There are videos, too. The videos accessible through the Grief's Journey website include the following:

- *Dealing with Grief at the Holidays,* which gives hope as well as advice on how to face special days after the death of a loved one.
- *Griefsong*—a video collection of songs by Paul Alexander. The songs, many of which are inspirational, are about the journey of grief.
- *Journey of Loss*—an interactive DVD, which challenges some beliefs about grief and bereavement and encourages motivation.
- *Till Human Voices Wake Us,* which depicts the effect of trauma and gives instructions for positive, guilt-free survival.

Also listed in the media section are magazines and magazine articles pertaining to bereavement.

Grief's Journey has a resources section that is excellent, and a home section through which members can participate in discussions every day, twenty-four hours a day. Membership is free.

Grief, Australia (www.grief.org.au/internetl.html)

This website is a nationally active nongovernmental organization in Australia that is dedicated to spreading education and awareness about the effects and experiences of living with grief. The organization often holds national and international conferences, lectures, and seminars related to bereavement. Australians can research locations of counseling centers or the next seminar. Even if you do not live in Australia you will benefit from the information, the helpful links, and a wide selection of publications.

Although the publications are largely aimed at health-care professionals, there are many resources available for the average bereaved person. Visitors to the website can subscribe to a vast library that includes everything from scientific studies about grief to children's fiction.

This is not an emotional support community. Instead, it is a site that provides information and resources about grief.

Hospice International (www.hospiceinternational.com)

Despite its name, Hospice International is an intimate site developed by Kim Hammer, a Canadian citizen, in memory of her sister Alison. Technically, Hospice International may be the most comprehensive international hospice site in cyberspace, covering countries in four continents, and offering hospice literature, services, and support in eight different languages. The site is a haven for Kim's stories and poetry about her lost loved ones. If you would like to submit your own poetry and stories, Kim will post them. You will find links to related websites about grief and loss.

National Cancer Institute: Loss, Grief, and Bereavement (www.cancer.gov/cancertopics/pdq/supportivecare/bereavement/ Patient/page1)

The United States' National Cancer Institute (NCI) offers this website for those who have lost a loved one from cancer. The website is split into two categories: one site for bereaved families and another for health-care professionals. The two halves mirror one another, offering similar information in layman's and professional language, respectively. In addition, there is a third site in Spanish.

The website is short and sweet, offering very broad, but helpful information. Some topics include complicated grief, children and grief, and stages of grief. Articles are written in an encyclopedic style and offer resources that are related specifically to the NCI.

Tragedy Assistance Program for Survivors (www.taps.org)

The Tragedy Assistance Program for Survivors (TAPS) is an extensive nonprofit organization developed in 1994 by the family members of eight soldiers killed in a National Guard aircraft tragedy in 1992. TAPS was developed as a support group for those who have lost their loved ones to military tragedies. Since 1994, TAPS has assisted more than twenty-five thousand grieving spouses, family members, and friends of American military troops killed in action.

The website offers a large online community, free of membership fees, where bereaved family members can post on messages boards and read articles and convention transcripts. There is also information on free counseling by the Department of Veteran Affairs in hundreds of locations.

In addition to online help, TAPS offers summer Good Grief Camps for children under age 21, as well as adult seminars in various places around the nation. In their own words, the TAPS Good Grief Camps provide children and teens "with a safe and supportive atmosphere to conduct activities and have opportunities to learn coping skills, establish and identify support systems and create awareness that they are not alone in the grief of their loved one." The adult seminars also have the mission of developing lifelong support networks among the families of fallen soldiers.

Prices for off-line programs are extremely affordable and often free. The site also provides links to every army, navy, air force, and marine grief service. Also, links are provided to various trauma services, governmental agencies, and even many members of the armed forces.

Bereaved Parents of the USA (www.bereavedparentsusa.org)

People who have lost someone to extreme violence have specific bereavement needs and this website caters to those needs. The site provides articles on legal issues surrounding murder as well as dealing with grief after a murder. This site is an informational site about Bereaved Parents of the USA, a self-help, not-for-profit organization. You will learn about its support groups and awareness programs. Additionally, the site gives useful links and has articles for the newly bereaved.

Here you can subscribe to the BP/USA newsletter, which is issued quarterly. The newsletter contains articles of interest to those grieving the loss of a child or grandchild and also includes helpful book reviews.

The Miss Foundation (www.missfoundation.org)

This foundation is for parents and extended family of a child who has died. There is an online support community as well as face-to-face support groups in certain cities. There is a newsletter and lots of information. There's even a downloadable funeral planner. The online forums contain twenty-seven online support groups with thousands of members. They also have workshops and a speaker list.

Beyond Indigo (www.beyondindigo.com)

There are forums here for folks who have lost a spouse, a parent, a child, a sibling, or a pet. The website also offers newsletters, plus opportunities to read personal stories or post your own stories and to engage in discussions about your loss and religion, holidays, and more. This website is known to academicians who are studying

the effects of grief and there are many research studies in which you can anony-
mously participate.

Solace After a Death (www.solaceafteradeath.com)
I have created this website for you, the reader of this book. Please visit the website
to listen to words of comfort and to find new ways to help yourself.

No matter your need, no matter your interest, no matter your predicament, there
is a website on the Internet that is designed to help you. Keep looking.

Blogs
A blog (Web log) is a posting on the Internet that can be a personal essay or
an ongoing journal. Anyone can write a blog and post it. That's the good
news—you can write and have your words read by people around the world.
You can express your sorrow, your grief, or your innermost feelings. Then
there's the bad news—the people posting on these blogs are not necessarily
professional people and sometimes may write something that is offensive or
misleading.

That said, you will benefit from reading what others have to say about
their bereavement experience, and then you can post your own comments
if you wish. People respond to one another's postings on these sites and offer encouragement, condolences, and information, too. You can be as
anonymous as you want to be. And that's where you must be careful because
someone may claim to be an expert about something or have a particular
experience and there is no way to verify the person's reports. So it's a good
idea to read blogs not for their facts or wisdom but for their poetry, their
emotional expression, and their humanity.

There are many sites on the Internet where anyone can create a free
blog, add color and music, and write freely with no editing or criticism.
Communities called "blogrings" ensure that these writings are easy for you
to locate on the Internet.

Below is a list of sites where you can create your own anonymous blog,
free of charge. These sites are geared toward the beginner blogger. If you
have no experience with Web design, these are the sites for you. Livejournal,
especially, is simple and easy to use.

- www.blogger.com—The traditional blog creator.
- www.myspace.com—Here, you can write a blog attached to a personal profile. You can add "friends" to your profile that facilitate social networking.
- www.livejournal.com—Livejournal is a blogging community with more privacy controls available than the traditional blog.
- http://wordpress.com/tag/bereavement—This is a website (Word Press.com) where you can write your own blog. This particular page on the above address on WordPress is strictly bereavement. Go to it—you'll be amazed at the number of videos, and most of them are excellent.

Here are some blogs created by individuals who are grieving the death of a loved one. Of course, since blogs are more informal than websites, they change subjects or even cease to exist at any point. Every time I've checked the blogs listed here, they've been just fine and rather useful, too. Some days the postings are simple and easy to read, and other days they are academic and stuffy. Sometimes people post heartbreaking videos and some days there are delightful poems. You never know what you will find on a blog. I have tried to choose blogs with some durability, and of course you can locate any blog about any topic by using a search engine.

The Grief Blog (www.thegriefblog.com)
The Grief Blog is a public blog where grieving individuals as well as professionals can post stories, poetry, and articles. The two administrators, Doctors Gloria and Heidi Horsley, are psychotherapists who often reply and give helpful tips and emotional support to their writers. Additionally, anyone reading the blog entries can comment.

MysteryORiley (www.mysteryoriley.wordpress.com)
Emmitt Owen Riley was two weeks short of his twenty-first birthday when his body was found in the Petaluma River in June 2007. Since then, Linda, his mother, has kept a blog tracking her own experiences with grief and loss. Linda calls her site: "A blog I never wanted to write." Of her site, Linda says that it is "a glimpse of how we're making it from day to day, to take you on this journey of

unbelievable grief, loss, and mystery. Not something everyone will care to do. But, there are other families who have experienced similar losses, and few know how to respond. Perhaps we can help in some way, just by sharing our thoughts and feelings."

Living Beyond Loss (www.adrr.com/living)
Between 1993 and 1997, Stephen R. Marsh and his wife buried three daughters. They created this Web page to share their experiences in dealing with grief and loss. The Marshes' essays about the deaths of their three children are brutal in their sincerity. Stephen Marsh continues to keep a blog (there is a link on the site) that talks about grief but also includes anecdotes and links for simple entertainment value. It is his way of getting through life one day at a time.

Widow's Quest (www.widowsquest.com)
Widow's Quest is a collage of posts by individuals dealing with the loss of a spouse. The posts range from affirmations of life to financial tips. Writers share pictures and videos found on the Internet and poetry even if it isn't their own. The site has archives dating back to January 2006 and continues to update to this day. Readers can post their own comments on any entry and writers often respond to them.

YouTube

YouTube.com (at www.youtube.com) is a website where anyone can create a video and put it up for all to see. It is easy to find everything from professional seminar videos to cartoons. Membership as well as viewing *any* video is entirely free. Because of this, YouTube.com is a revolution in information sharing. It is simple and easy to use, and links the average person with a wealth of information from all over the world.

When you click on the site there will be a box in which you can type in the subject of the video you are searching for. Simply type in "grief." You will have a choice of academic lectures, silly sympathy songs, heartfelt tributes, and hundreds of other grief-related videos. And you, too, can create a video and post it to www.youtube.com.

Listed next are some YouTube sites you might find interesting. When you get the video you want up on the screen, please note that there is a box on the right of the video screen that lists other videos on the same topic. You can click on them to get even more information.

Death of a Son: A Mother's Journey
(www.youtube.com/watch?v=o5HohuuPcs0)
This ten-minute video is the recorded testimony of a mother whose grown son Danny fell to his death as he was mountain climbing. The video goes through the various stages of grief as the mother talks about the ways she's dealt with those stages and has continued to live her life.

Do Not Stand at My Grave and Weep: Comfort in Grief
(www.youtube.com/watch?v=wxawiWqf4gA)
This video short is a poem turned inspirational movie. The moving words are set in front of beautiful pictures of nature and in the background plays music by Brady Barnett in memory of his son Jonah. The film is brought to you by TheLightBeyond.com.

Bereavement: The Psychology and Physiology of Loss
(www.youtube.com/watch?v=5ATG-lRduHI)
In this movie, Anita Sacks, a clinical instructor of psychiatry at New York University, discusses the clinical aspects of grief and bereavement. Her approach defines bereavement in a clinical manner and then discusses the effects that grief and bereavement can have on the body. This approach is less emotional and more academic than the preceding films.

SIRA: Grief and Bereavement
(www.youtube.com/watch?v=Qyt56m_3tNM)
This movie was developed by the University of California. It is an hour-long video of a seminar given by Sidney Zisook, M.D., a professor of psychiatry at UCSD. In this seminar, Dr. Zisook walks his audience through the different stages of grief from guilt to acceptance. It includes a discussion about acute grief and its connection to chronic clinical depression.

Bereavement (www.youtube.com/watch?v=uQQREszUIrY)
This three-minute short is a montage discussing emotions connected to the death of a loved one. It includes several interviews about grief and discusses the different ways in which grief is expressed in our society. It is brought to you by www.americanmontage.com.

Gifts of Grief (www.youtube.com/watch?v=o3AqWliYZNk)
This two-minute trailer is an advertisement for the film *Gifts of Grief,* which is a documentary that follows seven individuals as they cope with the deaths of family

members and close friends, and then discover the gifts they find along their journey. The film features interviews by Isabel Allende, Reverend Cecil Williams, Alana Laraine, Zen monk and Vietnam veteran Claude AnShin Thomas, and filmmaker Lee Mun Wah. Complete information on the film can be found at www.giftsofgrief.com.

The Amelia Center (www.youtube.com/watch?v=vRKrExD13SE)

This center was established in 1995, in Alabama, by the parents of Amelia Elliot, who was killed in a car accident. The center offers grief counseling, psychotherapy, networking, and other support for family members. It is a charitable organization run entirely on donations. As you surf the Internet, you will note that there are many such local centers and they each have produced a promotional video similar to this one.

You may also wish to check out:

- http://thelightbeyond.typepad.com. The subtitle of this site is "You are not alone in your grief."
- www.youngwidowsandwidowers.com
- www.respectance.com
- www.dailystrength.org

Enjoy the Internet. It is your always available friend, ready to serve you every day and every night.

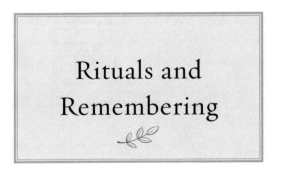

CHAPTER 5

Rituals and Remembering

You and your family will decide which rituals help you. You may welcome certain memorial rites now and others many months from now. There is no timetable to follow. Simply do whatever helps you.

FUNERALS

Traditionally, people would buy cemetery grave lots or plots or would buy mausoleum space far in advance of death. Today, a growing number of people purchase their funerals in advance, too. Financially, the consumer is protected because funeral funds cannot be accessed by the funeral home until it is proven that a death has occurred. Emotionally, the family of the deceased is protected because they don't have to write a check on the day their loved one dies. When you are prepaying your funeral, most funeral homes encourage you to have an estate planner or attorney review your contracts with them. This is not usually possible when relatives go into a funeral home for the first time on the day of a death.

When preplanning their funeral, many people arrange for the funeral to be a celebration. Still others plan their memorial service and specify the music to be played, the speaker who will deliver the eulogy, and the menu, too. I recently attended such an event. It was held in a catering hall. The deceased

arranged for everyone to go there after the religious service. She had chosen the food and drink and the arrangement of the tables. It was a party to
honor her life.

Funerals are important. In *Parallel Time*, journalist Brent Staples writes,
"The rituals of grief and burial bear the dead away. Cheat those rituals and
you risk keeping the dead with you and always in forms that you might not
like. Choose carefully the funerals you miss."

No matter the type of funeral you had for your loved one, know that funerals are psychologically good for you. They give you the tangible proof
that the person is gone. They prevent you from having fantasies that the person will return. You were there and you witnessed the funeral. This is helpful in your recovery from bereavement.

Suggestions from a Young Widower in Rochester, New York

*We were only married for two years and when I had to find clothes to bury
my wife in I chose her wedding gown. I'm glad I did that. I recommend it.*

Remember to call on your funeral director if you run into difficulties; he
or she is trained to help you.

Cremation

These days, funeral directors know how to deal with cremation. The number
of cremations increases annually—almost one-third of funeral services are
now cremations. Some people choose cremation because their family members may be living throughout the country, or the world; thus a local, home-
town cemetery has no meaning to them. Relatives will not be around town,
dropping in to the cemetery to visit the grave site.

Others may choose cremation because it costs far less than a traditional
burial. But, that is true only if the ashes are scattered in a simple ceremony.
There are companies that specialize in packing ashes into fireworks for a
splashy display and companies that float the ashes up in balloons. Charles M.
Chafer is a high-tech entrepreneur and a pioneer of the commercial space

age. He is the chief executive officer of Space Services Inc., a company that provides opportunities for the public to participate in space missions, and his company has delivered cremated remains into outer space by rocket.

Some people turn to cremation as a way of personalizing their final moment and expressing their interests in a unique fashion. A fisherman planned a cruise for his friends and asked to have them scatter his ashes while out at sea. A terminally ill woman who is adventurous, but afraid of heights, has asked that her friends take a hot-air balloon ride, something she has wanted to do but is too fearful to undertake, and throw her ashes down from above.

After a cremation the ashes, called cremains, can be kept in an urn, can be buried in a cemetery plot, or can be scattered either by the family or by the crematory. Many crematories have what they call scattering gardens just for this purpose. Of course, if you wish to keep the ashes at home with you that is perfectly fine, too.

I attended a wedding where it was known that the groom's father had recently died. After the minister completed the ceremony, and the "I do's" were said, the groom removed a vial from his pocket. He showed the assembled guests that it was filled with ashes and expressed appreciation that his dad was represented at his wedding.

Jane E. Brody, the *New York Times's* Personal Health columnist, has written that "a traditional funeral and in-ground burial is not my choice. . . . I would rather the many thousands of dollars such a finale can cost go directly to my heirs or a cause I support, and I would rather my body be used to better the world, say, through donation to a medical school."

Green Burials

Some funeral homes now offer green burials. Green burials, meant to preserve the environment, have no coffin or casket and no embalming. In a natural state, the deceased is wrapped in a shroud and buried in the ground. Trees, not granite or marble stones, are used as place markers. (See www .greenburialcouncil.org.) Green burials mimic almost six thousand years of Jewish tradition, which states that Jews should be buried directly in the ground or in simple pine caskets. The caskets should decompose the same way remains would decompose and there should be no embalming.

Eulogies

Eulogies are tributes to the deceased. Once, eulogies were delivered by a stern clergyman who may or may not have known the deceased. But nowadays, members of the family, friends, neighbors, and colleagues, too, are asked to contribute to the service. When the funeral service is personalized and family-run, a true portrait of the deceased person is brought to light.

Philip Melville, a young husband whose wife died of pancreatic cancer, spoke at her funeral with his four young children beside him. Here is an excerpt from his eulogy:

> "I weep for my love. I stand before you with my heart in shreds, every word like glass in my throat. Rochelle was my north, my south, my east, and my west. . . . Every morning I told her I could not possibly love her any more and every night I did."

Amy, a young woman whose mother died of lymphoma, spoke at her funeral. She told her fellow mourners:

> "My mother was an extraordinary patient. She was the first patient in the history of the stem-cell transplant unit at New York Presbyterian Hospital to ask for an exercise bicycle in her room. This inspired the physical therapy department to apply for a grant for six exercise bikes, which have now become a permanent part of the unit."

At another funeral, a son recalled parts of his mother's life:

> "Helen and a neighbor frequently walked the Hollywood hills at a brisk pace before dawn, meeting and checking their lap times on her large wristwatch. Both octogenarians strived to improve their pace, but sometimes just walked without a goal. Helen took yoga classes at the local Y, practiced headstands, tai chi, and meditation. She and her husband, Sy, willed their bodies to science for use by the next generation of doctors and people who, like they, are fascinated by the

wonders and beauty of life. Her epitaph was difficult to put into simple words, but ends with her biggest gift: 'Humanitarian.'"

A middle-age daughter spoke at her mother's funeral as follows:

"My father died of a heart attack, just short of his forty-first birthday. My mother was thirty-seven. It was a devastating, monumental, cataclysmic event. Wherever we thought we were going, we were now going somewhere else. This was an era when women had little economic power and day care was unheard of. My mother was deeply grieved and appeared completely overcome. My maternal grandmother tried her best to run our household. After about three weeks, my mother emerged from seclusion. She calmly announced that we had to get on with our lives and she started on a plan, step by step. And we all got on with our lives. Her life teaches us that it does not matter how overwhelmed we may feel. It is okay to feel scared. What matters is what we do about the problem."

A young mother reminisced about her father at his funeral:

"Many people go through this world living ordinary lives. They work at ordinary jobs, raise their families, and live out their last years in quiet retirement. My father was not one of these people. He lived a fascinating, rich, and purposeful life, one that was at times fraught with pain and sacrifice. He was not, as my mother often said, easy to get along with. He was opinionated, stubborn, and as tough on himself as he was on others. He was a passionate man who loved a good sausage and strudel, appreciated art and history and philosophy; he loved to dance and waltz and sing loudly. He has left his mark on all of us."

A young dad delivered the eulogy for his infant son, who died seventeen weeks after birth, never having left the hospital. The dad wanted family and friends to know about the baby. He described the baby's face and body, he named the songs that he and his wife sang to their baby, and he made the sounds that put a smile on the baby's face. At the end of the service, all mourners felt they knew that infant whom they had never seen.

Consider sending copies of eulogies spoken about your loved one to younger family members, along with your beloved's photo. These will become important keepsakes and a significant part of family history for generations to come.

If you need help writing a eulogy or a remembrance speech, please go to www.solaceafteradeath.com.

MOURNING CUSTOMS

Much of your bereavement response will depend on the culture you are in. Every group mourns in its own fashion. A few cultures believe that mourning should last a lifetime and those mourners have no expectation of recovery. You will express your pain in a way that is compatible not only with your personality but also with your particular culture.

In twenty-first century America, wakes are traditional gatherings held after the death and before the funeral. The wake may be in the home of the deceased or at the funeral home. Often, there is feasting and drinking, but sometimes it is simply a viewing and an opportunity to say good-bye to the deceased in a formal farewell. Wakes provide an opportunity for family bonding, particularly in these days of far-flung families.

Centuries ago, the purpose of a wake was to guarantee that the person was really dead. Mourners at the viewing were instructed to look for possible signs of life.

Whereas wakes are a Christian tradition, *shivah* is a Jewish tradition. Jewish families sit shivah for seven days, beginning right after the burial. The blood relatives of the deceased unite—if possible, in the home of the deceased—and accept visitors from morning to night. The family members do not leave the house, except to go to synagogue, and do not participate in any social or business events. There is no entertaining. They are not to wear new clothes or listen to music. Instead, they simply receive guests and reminisce about their loved one.

In the Philippines the more emotion expressed, the more respectful the mourner is thought to be. Grief is encouraged and some believe that grief reactions should last forever. It is not unusual for a widow, or for a mother whose child has died, to wear black every day for the rest of her life. In some remote areas of Portugal, Spain, and Greece, too, widows will wear mourning garb for the rest of their lives.

If you live in Egypt, you are expected to grieve in public and extreme emotional expression is encouraged. Men, as well as women, display deep feelings—keeping a stiff upper lip is deemed ridiculous. For days, or sometimes weeks, mourners will wail and beat their chests. Sometimes the mourners are people who have been hired to wail and beat their chests, to show the community that the family is feeling extreme loss.

In Bali, you laugh and enjoy yourself when a loved one dies because the entire community comes over to distract you with jokes. They all will insist that you be joyful. Weeping over someone who died is discouraged and calmness is encouraged. They believe that the death is God's will, and if you grieve excessively, you are going against God's will. Suffering after a death is considered detrimental to the community and to the mourner. The Balinese believe that the soul of the deceased is affected by the actions of the living; thus, the negative energy of grief is discouraged.

In many small towns in Japan, the dead remain part of their family's daily life. In the home there is an altar, or shrine, to the deceased family ancestors. The dead person's photos are above the shrine and family members pray and offer gifts of food and drink, as well as conversation, to the dead person at that altar. The ceremonies surrounding deaths and memorial services are quite elaborate. The body is dressed in an expensive white kimono and given paper money that is thought to be useful in the afterlife. The Japan Consumers' Association reports that the average funeral costs $21,500. Japanese ancestor worship has lessened in more recent years, especially in big cities. Yet, mourners who continue to follow their cultural traditions usually recover from grief quicker, and experience less depression and anxiety, than do those who do not adhere to their cultural norms.

In India, Hindus have a strong belief in reincarnation, believing that people are reborn into higher forms of life. The belief that the person will enter a better world upon dying encourages that dying person to be strong. The Hindu death ceremony can last as long as twelve days. Those days are filled with religious chants, drums, bells, and special prayers. Incense is burned until the rooms are filled with smoke. The body is adorned with new clothes and expensive perfumes. Some Hindus believe that expressions of grief can hinder the soul's transformation, so outward expressions of grief are not encouraged.

In Ethiopia, both men and women express their emotions outwardly to demonstrate their grief. They will cry and beat their chests until they are in pain. After the funeral both men and women shave their heads and wear black. Some northern Ethiopians will scratch their faces with a thorny fruit to show their grief. In Sierra Leone, men are expected to stay with one another and drink, but not cry. The women are expected to join together, as well, but they are told that they must cry.

The Lakota tribe of Native Americans encourages friends and family to put a memento into the casket. This is considered a sign of love and respect. The Lakota believe that the spirit of the deceased stays around for about a year. The closest relatives wrap a lock of the deceased's hair in buckskin to symbolize the spirit. They protect that spirit from harsh weather, and feed it daily for a year. When the year is over, there is a celebration that includes an exchange of gifts and a feast.

In Korea, relatives who were present at the moment of death are expected to express their grief by wailing. The more a child wails, the more faithful that child is considered. Koreans wear white when they are in mourning and the body stays in the home for about a week. During the day, food is offered to the soul of the dead and the extended family stays together for that week.

You will be most comfortable practicing the grief customs of your community. Your religious leader or your local funeral home director can help you figure out just what is best for you to do.

MONUMENTS

Memorial stones are solid evidence of both the life and the death of your beloved. You may want to make the monument the focus of your mourning and regularly visit the cemetery.

Just as some people plan their funeral, some others decide what they would like to have inscribed on their monument, also called a tombstone or gravestone. In some ethnic groups, a photo of the deceased is attached to the monument. An epitaph is a brief statement commemorating a deceased person; the epitaph usually is engraved on the monument.

Here are some epitaphs written by folks who planned ahead:

John in Ruidoso, New Mexico, requested a pun be imprinted on his monument:

"Here lies Johnny Yeast
Pardon me for not rising."

New Englanders are reputed to shun the spotlight. Representing Stowe, Vermont's, reticence, this anonymous New Englander asked for the following inscription:

"I was somebody.
Who, is no business of yours."

And in a cemetery in Georgia were found the following last words:

"I told you I was sick."

Some disgruntled spouses got the last word by writing their mate's epitaphs:

"Here lies the body of Mary Devoe
Wife of Henry Devoe
Tears cannot bring her back
Therefore I weep."

"Beneath this stone
My wife doth lie
Now she's at rest
And so am I."

"Anna Wallace
The children of Israel wanted bread
And the Lord sent them manna,
Old clerk Wallace wanted a wife,
And the Devil sent him Anna."

Probably some glib relatives or friends wrote the following:

"Here lies Ezekiel Aikle
~ Age 102 ~
The Good Die Young."

"Henry Edsel Smith
Born 1903—Died 1942
Looked up the elevator shaft to see if
the car was on the way down. It was."

"Here lies the body
of Jonathan Blake
Stepped on the gas
Instead of the brake."

The banker in my town insists that he loves his job so much his monument will read: I WAS AT WORK YESTERDAY.

Of course, most epitaphs are not humorous but rather polite and proper, attempting to describe the person in just a few adjectives. There aren't too many families who appreciate a sarcastic or humorous epitaph. Most people prefer a solemn reminder.

It is important to have tangible reminders of the deceased, and memorial stones can serve that purpose. They also designate a specific spot where mourners can congregate, reminisce, weep, and perhaps talk to their loved one. Whenever you are at the cemetery and see the monument, which is a testament to your loved one, it is perfectly appropriate and acceptable for you to weep.

ANNIVERSARY DAYS

Please do not be alarmed by occasional setbacks. Special days bring up special feelings. Days that are joyful may be tearful, too. Holidays, birthdays, graduations, weddings, family celebrations, and anniversary days can be difficult. Anniversary days include the anniversary of the death or of the diagnosis or of a special event you shared with the deceased. An anniversary day might be your beloved's birthday or wedding anniversary. It is normal and appropriate to experience an unhappy anniversary reaction.

> *Suggestions from a Mother in Connecticut*
>
> *If your only child passed away, tell your family you want to celebrate Mother's Day anyway. My first childless Mother's Day was horrible. Everyone in my family was afraid they would upset me so they acted as if it was not Mother's Day. Of course, I knew what day it was. I upset myself but it would have been easier if someone said, "Happy Mother's Day." After all, I was a mother for fourteen years.*

Many of my clients report that after the first year of bereavement they are symptom-free except for anniversary days. And for some people those painful feelings tend to reappear every year during the anniversary days.

Rose Fitzgerald Kennedy, commenting on her anniversary reaction to the death of her son, President John F. Kennedy, once stated, "It has been said, 'Time heals all wounds.' I do not agree. The wounds remain. In time, the mind, protecting its sanity, covers them with scar tissue and the pain lessens. But, it is never gone."

Anniversary reactions are so widespread that most religions have a formalized ritual to follow on the anniversary of the death. There may be a particular prayer or a memorial candle-lighting ceremony. That ritual provides a formalized way to discharge extra emotions. Look to your religion for guidelines.

Personal Rituals

Some people prefer to revise their established religious guidelines to better suit themselves, their family, and their lifestyle. Other people actually create their own rituals to mark the anniversary. Please find a way to prepare for the anniversary days. You can create a ritual that will be easy for you to bear and will provide you with some comfort, too.

I know a family whose grandmother loved to bake. She supplied cookies and cakes, pies and pastries, for every intergenerational family get-together. When she died, each adult child and each grandchild took it upon themselves to learn to bake a particular treat that Grandma used to make. Annually, at the anniversary of Grandma's death, they all get together. Although they are spread throughout the United States, they meet at one central location to share their goodies and to reminisce.

Some ideas for personal rituals are to:

- Volunteer at a place that reminds you of your loved one. Do this on an anniversary day.
- Organize an annual anniversary day outing with the same group of people each year. If the deceased dad enjoyed sports, the family and friends might attend a ball game in his memory. I have a client whose late husband was an actor. On the anniversary of his death, the entire clan congregates to enjoy an evening of theater.
- Bring flowers to a particular place on the anniversary day. It could be the cemetery or it might be a nursing home or senior center or maybe even a day-care center. Decide on a place that would have meaning to your loved one.
- Hold an annual memorial service and invite guests to bring original poetry as well as family photos and videos.
- Exchange gifts with family members on the evening before the anniversary of the death.
- Select a song that celebrates the life your beloved enjoyed. Teach the words to a group of friends or family.

Each of the suggested rituals listed here engages you to act. That's a good thing. Too much passivity during dark days only gets you brooding. The activities outlined in the previous list will help you connect with other people. That, too, is a good thing. Having a prescribed ritual gives you some certainty. There's no room for floundering when you must undertake a specific action. At this time of your life, you need all the certainty you can find. Choose your unique life-affirming ritual. It will help you heal.

As the years go by, the annual ritual may be a good thing that holds the family together. Or, it may dwindle in importance and after serving its purpose for some years may no longer be necessary.

MEMORIAL CELEBRATIONS

Memorial celebrations may be held weeks or months after the death. This permits time for planning and time for out-of-towners to arrange their schedules. There is usually some kind of entertainment or presentation, and sometimes there is food, as well. I was at a memorial service where the adult grandchildren sang an original song that they wrote in their grandfather's memory. I attended a memorial service for a young woman who loved dogs at which all attendees were invited to bring their dogs.

When my mother died, my sister and I each held a tribute to her in our respective homes. We told anecdotes and stories, and our guests were given song sheets when they walked in. Later in the ceremony, we explained each song's significance in our mother's life and then invited all guests to sing along. Our mother's life was celebrated.

Poetry is popular at memorial celebrations and guests appreciate receiving a copy of a poem favored by the deceased. Using a computer, you can create a memorial document with photos, poetry, and more. Your guests will take that document home and always remember your loved one. If you need help planning a memorial celebration, see www.solaceafteradeath.com.

CHAPTER 6

Helping Children Through Grief

Few families discuss death as a part of their children's educational and social agenda. Parents much prefer pretending death does not exist, and who can blame us? All parents want to protect their offspring from hurt, sadness, and fear. It's that urge to protect that sends parents to the pet shop to replace the dead goldfish they flushed away while their child was in school.

Imagine for a moment that the child did come home from school and see pet Goldy floating in the fish tank. Yes, the child would be upset. Yes, the child would cry. And yes, the child would soon get over it. The child would have proof that he or she could face death, weep in mourning, and then recover. That is not a bad lesson to learn.

The luckiest children are those whose first experiences of human death are people on whom they were not dependent. A distant relative, a friend's parent, or a former neighbor are relationships that are not crucial to the child. It isn't that these deaths are unimportant. Rather, it is that it is easier to experience death from a distance than it is for a child to suffer the loss of a close relative. Do not shelter your children; allow them to know about these deaths. Your children will then know that they can deal with death and still be okay. This creates a model for successfully coping with subsequent deaths.

How much should children know? As much as they want to know.

When your child asks a question, please answer it and answer truthfully. Children are remarkably sensitive to the feelings of the adults in their lives. Kids know when you are telling the truth. Kids know when information is being withheld. The child in your life will figure out and respond to your unstated feelings. As soon as you can accept the death and speak about it, your child will relax and feel much better.

Children more readily accept the finality of death when they have attended the funeral or visited the cemetery. The usual reason why children are likely to be frightened at a funeral is because they may witness grown-ups being out of control. It may be the first time that the child has ever seen a parent, or any adult for that matter, crying. If a child has always depended on the adults in the family to be strong and to help her when she's in a jam, imagine how frightened she will be when she is experiencing the death of a loved one and all her other loved ones are unavailable to her because they are wailing and weeping. I recommend that a close friend or family member be assigned to stay with a child throughout the funeral service.

LISTENING TO YOUR CHILDREN

The more you speak about the death, the more likely you will clarify circumstances and clear up misconceptions. Pay careful attention to everything your children say after they have experienced a death. The Michaels family of Long Island, New York, told journalist Michael Winerip that soon after the death of their son Justin the family was driving and their surviving son said, "I have a brainstorm. If we crash the van right now, we could all go to heaven and see Justin again." It was immediately apparent that plenty more conversations and discussions were necessary.

Among the misconceptions that I've heard from children in my practice are the following:

• *The death occurred because of something I did.*
Timmy punched a boy in his class during a recess fight. That boy died from an asthma attack several weeks later. Timmy thought he was responsible for the death.

- *The death occurred because of something I secretly wished.*

Marcia was angry because her dad forbade her to wear a particular dress to her middle-school graduation party. He thought the dress was too provocative. Marcia thought he was totally wrong and wished he would disappear. When he died of an unexpected heart attack, she worried that her wish was responsible for the death. I had to convince her that if her wishes were so powerful she would be able to wish him to return.

- *The death occurred because of something I said.*

Nick knew that his parents had to go to the hospital to be with his very sick brother, but he hated staying home with a babysitter or with Grandpa. On one of his brother's last days Nick shouted, as his parents walked out the door, "I wish Paul would die already. Then you could stay home with me." When Paul died, Nick asked me if his words had caused the death.

- *If I tried harder I might have been able to save her.*

Sean's elderly grandmother lived with his family and suffered a stroke while watching television one evening. While the family was waiting for the ambulance, Sean tried getting a response from his grandmother, but she was nonresponsive. When the emergency technicians arrived at the house, Sean wanted to continue his efforts. They insisted she had to be placed on the stretcher and go right to the hospital. He thought if he had persisted she would have lived.

- *Soon it will be my turn to die.*

Until he heard the announcement in school that one of the students in his shop class had lost his battle with cancer, Alec didn't realize that a child could die. Once he knew that was in the realm of possibility, Alec became fearful that he, too, would die.

- *Soon everyone in my family will die and I will be alone.*

Within a period of four months Michael's two grandfathers passed away. One died from a heart attack and the other from prostate cancer. Michael worried that his parents and his grandmothers would soon follow.

- *The dead person is floating up in the sky and I will see him when my family flies to Disneyland.*

Airline personnel report that they often see youngsters peering out the plane windows looking for loved ones. Children do take things literally and when told that someone is "up in heaven," they easily interpret clouds as heavenly.

• *Everyone is saying that the good die young, so I won't be good anymore.*
In the movie *Yours, Mine, and Ours,* Lucille Ball is a young widow who reprimands her son for misbehaving. He replies, "But you told me God takes those who are good. I don't want God to take me."

SPEAKING TO YOUR CHILDREN

Children may need to be shown evidence that illness does not usually cause death. We all get sick and we then recover; health is a natural state. It is the rare exception who succumbs to disease. Bereaved children, like some bereaved adults, sometimes believe that they have the same symptoms as the deceased. Please explain to the child that it is possible to have those similar symptoms and yet live a full and long life.

Tell the truth. Use the word *dead.* That is the truth and it prevents the child from imagining that the person will soon return. It helps the child adjust to the finality of the situation. To say that the deceased is in a deep sleep may create future bedtime difficulties. To say that the deceased is away on a long trip may create separation difficulties. You don't want to encourage hope that the person will return. You do want to encourage hope that the child will once again be enthusiastic about life.

A client once told me:

"When I was a little girl, I overheard my mother talking with a neighbor. The neighbor said, 'Too bad she lost her mother.' It took me weeks before I was brave enough to ask my mother how that could have happened. During those weeks, I worried and refused to be separated from my mother for anything. I even followed her to the bathroom. I was petrified I would lose her."

Engage in family projects to help your child. Draw pictures of the deceased person, write a story about the person, or write a poem or a song. Assemble a photograph album or an online slide show of favorite photos. Such emotional expression is extremely helpful to children—and to you, too.

Talk about the deceased and about your feelings. Don't pretend that he never existed. State that you are sad and miss the person. Don't pretend that you are perfectly fine. When you are engaged in a family activity and miss your loved one, tell the kids how much you miss him. If you are thinking of him, they, too, are thinking of him.

It's okay to say, "This steak is delicious, Dad would surely have liked it" or "Sometimes I miss him so much that I think I see him in the street." Every feeling that you articulate comforts a child because you are giving the child permission to have those same feelings.

Children need tender sympathy. When President Lincoln's friend, who was a lieutenant colonel in the Civil War, was killed in battle, Lincoln wrote a letter to the officer's daughter. When you read the letter, written in 1862, you realize that no matter the century, children need concern and compassion, kindness and hope.

Dear Fanny,

It is with deep grief that I learn of the death of your kind and brave Father; and, especially, that it is affecting your young heart beyond what is common in such cases.

In this sad world of ours, sorrow comes to all; and, to the young, it comes with bitterest agony, because it takes them unawares. The older have learned to ever expect it.

I am anxious to afford some alleviation of your present distress. Perfect relief is not possible, except with time. You can not now realize that you will ever feel better. Is not this so? And yet it is a mistake. You are sure to be happy again. To know this, which is certainly true, will make you some less miserable now.

I have had experience enough to know what I say; and you need only to believe it, to feel better at once. The memory of your dear Father, instead of an agony, will yet be a sad sweet feeling in your heart, of a purer and holier sort than you have known before.

Please present my kind regards to your afflicted mother.

Your sincere friend,
A. Lincoln

Unlike an adult, who begins the bereavement process right after a death, a child takes a bit longer to start on her journey through bereavement. She may not begin mourning until she is assured that her needs for survival will be taken care of. A child's dependent status is strongly felt during bereavement.

She may actually behave or speak in ways that test her environment, in an attempt to assure herself that she will be taken care of. Thus, a previously compliant child may become stubborn. A sweet child may speak rudely. These children are testing you. Will you still love me? Will you still be here for me? Or, will you be like that other person I loved so much and disappear?

Children often are accused of being selfish after the death of a loved one because rather than speak about their loss they will speak about themselves and their needs. The newly bereaved child may ask, "But who will take me to the circus?" or "Who will take me shopping for my prom dress?" or "Now, how am I going to learn how to fish?" Once confident that their needs will be attended to, children resume their pre-bereavement behavior. And then, later, begin their mourning.

Until this point in her short life, your child has been encouraged to act grown up, be brave, and not give in to tears and fears when things go wrong. Now she needs plenty of time to gain the courage to risk feeling the depth of her loss. Please don't condemn or criticize a child for caring about her personal needs at the time of a family tragedy. That child is responding exactly as a child should. Permitting the child to feel the loss when she's ready for those strong feelings will allow her to experience mastery. Mastering her emotions will increase her coping ability for the rest of her life. She will never feel afraid of going out of control. She will know she can get through a difficult experience.

Wendy Schoenbach remembers what it felt like to be eleven years old and suddenly fatherless:

WENDY'S STORY

My father died abruptly and without warning from a heart attack in the middle of the night at home after a family gathering at our house. My brothers and I slept through the whole drama. I awoke the next morning to learn that my life in the wonderful place that we had lived in for barely a year had involuntarily changed irrevocably and forever.

When I learned that my father had died, at first I was in shock. I could not react. I did not cry. In later weeks, I was cranky and temperamental. I was in constant pain. I insisted on wearing a red wool baseball cap to school because it had been a recent gift from my father.

My brothers and I learned from our struggles, and in the end were stronger for it. However, we never felt anything but total devastation about our father's death. We felt so strongly that we did not dare speak of his death or of him, for fear of being overwhelmed and debilitated by the intense pain. If we had not buried our grief and turned away from it, we could not have functioned at school or at home. It was 1952. There was not much understanding of the bereavement of children then. There was no grief therapy then. No one knew what to say to us.

I became accustomed to the pain and believed that being a little sad was normal in life. I became accustomed to waking up with a heavy feeling that had to be overcome in order to get up, get dressed, and get going.

As I grew older, I always felt different from others. I looked at life through a sad lens. My brothers and I were more cautious, subdued, and pessimistic than our peers. We had been inwardly scarred and immediately and completely engulfed in fears. Forever shattered was the fundamental belief that every child takes for granted, the belief that we were safe and secure in our home under the protection of our parents. If my father could die at night in his bed, seemingly for no reason and without warning, then could not the same thing happen, at any time and without warning, to my mother?

UNDERSTANDING YOUR CHILDREN

Some children seem to not care about the death of a loved one. They don't cry, they don't act out, they don't even seem sad. Some kids act as if nothing unusual has happened. This indifference is usually the child's way of building up the courage to mourn. It is the mental preparation necessary before mourning can begin.

Young children try out different ways of connecting to a deceased loved one. They may talk to him, study his photos, keep special items that belonged to him, and frequently dream about him. Many children believe that the dead person, particularly if it is a parent, is watching them.

Michael told me:

"My father died when I was in fifth grade. Whenever I took a test in school, up until I took my last college final, I thought my father was in the room with me, encouraging me and worried about whether or not I would do well. I definitely felt his presence and even though it is irrational I still insist he was there with me."

When a parent dies, be sure no one tells the child that now he, or she, is the man, or woman, of the house. It's tragic that a parent was taken away from the child; don't intensify that tragedy by taking away the child's childhood, too. It's childhood that permits the child to be dependent and to get care and cuddling.

Researchers tell us that children in healthy families recover well and do not get overwhelmed by their loss. They do not have more psychological problems than do children who never had a death in their family. In a retrospective study of college women who had lost a parent years earlier, researchers found that although the women felt their lives had changed after the death, none reported that their lives were particularly troubled or filled with problems.

The best predictors of a child's recovery from grief are relationships with family members and with school friends. When those relationships are good, the outcome of grief is good.

Of course, if you are the surviving parent you must do what you can to continue parenting. The child has lost one parent to death. You do not want him to lose the other to grief.

🌿 Suggestions from Wendy in Massachusetts

If you are young when you lost a parent, like I was, look for another adult beside your other parent to spend some time with. I was still a child when my father died. If I had the power to change one aspect of my grieving process, I would have had one family member (other than my mother), preferably female, who called, wrote, or in some way communicated to me that she was there for me. I would have wanted her to say that she realized that it was awful and that there was nothing that she could ever say or do that would reverse the event. I wish that this person would have told me that she would always be there to talk to or maybe do things with now and again. I would then have known that there was someone who knew I was going through hell, who would listen, and who did in fact care about me. Some religions name "godparents" for their children. I think that this concept is good because it puts two people in place for situations like this. 🌿

CHAPTER 7

Novel Ways to Help Yourself

Throughout bereavement please mourn the way you need to mourn, the way that is comforting for you. Soon you will reorient your life toward the future. Your appetite and your sleep will return. Your energy will come back. Your ability to function all day long will resurface.

THE TAPPING CURE

In addition to the helpful instructions in the preceding pages there are two specialized techniques that bereaved people find particularly useful: *the tapping cure* and *visualizations*. Visualizations are covered in the next section of this chapter.

The tapping cure is a method of self-help, somewhat similar to acupressure. It does not use medication and does not use talk therapy. It requires that you tap, with your fingers, on particular points of your body while at the same time speaking about what is bothering you. Tapping can eliminate your feelings of distress. It can get rid of the negative feelings that you associate with certain thoughts. Tapping separates a painful emotion from a specific thought. So, you can still have the thoughts but they won't make you feel so bad. In fact, they won't make you feel bad at all.

Researchers are trying to figure out how the tapping technique accomplishes its feat. We know it works but we're not quite sure precisely why and how it works. The hypotheses range from theories that explain acupuncture to theories that explain psychotherapy. I suggest you try the method. You have nothing to lose but a few minutes and everything to gain.

To begin the tapping cure, I'd like you to use four fingers of either hand to tap on the following spots.

1. *The bone underneath your eye.* Either eye is okay. This is a useful tapping spot for bereavement.
2. *The junction of your nose and your inner eyebrow.* Try tapping on that spot with one or two fingers.
3. *Your collarbone.* Using both hands, tap your fingers on each side of your collarbone.
4. *Your side, midway between your waist and your underarm.* For this spot you can use either hand and either side of your body.
5. *The cuticle of your pinky* so that your finger touches some of your finger and some of your nail.
6. *On top of your hand, in-between your pinky and your ring finger.* Tap with four fingers for this one. So, if you are right handed, you'll place your right hand on top of your left hand. The pinky of your right hand will be in-between the pinky and ring finger of your left hand. The other fingers of your right hand will simply be on top of the left hand. It will seem as if your right index finger is almost at your left wrist.

Although there are many other tapping spots on your hands and your face, the six spots I've just introduced are usually the most efficient when it comes to bereavement issues. Try this now: tap on your eyebrow spot, under eye spot, collarbone, your side, your pinky spot, and then the spot on top of your hand. Do this several times until you know the spots well. You are halfway there.

The second half of this healing exercise is to figure out what to say while tapping. You repeat one sentence aloud while tapping on each spot. As you move from spot to spot, you repeat your sentence. To formulate your sentence think of a few words or a phrase to describe your worst feelings. Among the phrases selected by some of my bereaved clients are the following:

- I am very lonely.
- My best friend is gone.
- Her chair is still empty.
- I hate sleeping alone in our king-size bed.
- I feel a hole in my heart.

Please write your sentence. Your sentence should describe the situation that is the most painful to you, the situation that is disturbing your life today. If nothing is terribly distressing you today, then today you do not need to perform the tapping cure. If you are in distress, then write your sentence now.

Then tack the following two words onto the beginning of your sentence: "Even though." Good. Now add the following words to the end of your sentence: "I can handle it."

So, if your original sentence was "I am miserable because I miss my beloved very, very much," your complete sentence would now be, "Even though I am miserable because I miss my beloved very, very much I can handle it."

Here are some other possibilities for the sentence endings:

- I'll soon be over it.
- I am looking ahead, not back.
- I have a good life ahead of me.
- I will soon be okay.
- I can act like it's no big deal.
- I accept myself.
- I love myself.
- I am lovable.

Decide which sentence ending is most appropriate for you and tack it onto the end of your sentence. Here are some sentences that might be useful to you:

- Even though her chair is still empty, I accept myself.
- Even though I am terribly lonely, I will be fine very soon.
- Even though I miss my mom, I know I am lovable.
- Even though I am sad now, I can still do what must be done.
- Even though I feel like my life is over, I know I will soon recover.
- Even though I am afraid, I accept myself.
- Even though I am angry at him for dying, I love myself.
- Even though he left me at a terrible time, I will get back to myself.
- Even though life is so unfair, I accept myself.
- Even though I have buried my son, I will go on living.

Looking down at the paper on which you have written your completed sentence, you can now begin your tapping. Please tap on each spot while you say your sentence. Then pause, take a deep breath, and notice how you feel. Probably, you will feel much better and much less upset. You might want to repeat the tapping sequence a few times—after all, it takes less than a minute to do all of the taps.

Pay attention to yourself and your feelings while you tap and decide if one or two of the tapping spots are more effective than the others. Then, decide if one or two of the spots seem to have no effect. Now you can personalize your tapping protocol to suit yourself. You might want to eliminate one or two spots and concentrate on others and go through your tapping routine once more. By this time, you should be feeling much better. Test yourself by thinking of your original situation and notice your reaction to it. It doesn't bother you anymore, right? You did a good job.

You can use tapping for the relief of grief symptoms and throughout your life to help you with other burdens and overwhelming feelings. Feelings of abandonment, anger, betrayal, loneliness, and boredom respond well to the tapping cure.

Some people tap every morning to start their day. Others tap before bedtime. Some tap for a few consecutive days and then never need to again tap because they have mastered their situation. Some tap in anticipation of a difficult time ahead—that is, right before a visit to certain people or on the anniversary of the death.

You will obtain your best results if you do your tapping at a time when you are extremely emotional and very much in distress.

For more information about tapping, look for books and websites that further explain it. One of the books is called *The Tapping Cure* and I am the author of it. You can buy it at bookstores or at Amazon.com or from www.solaceafteradeath.com.

VISUALIZATIONS THAT HEAL

The process of visualizing specific images, sometimes referred to as *guided imagery*, is a self-help method. It is a method that permits you to use your mind to help you feel better and function at a more efficient, effective level. You actually visualize a helpful image in your mind and then your brain absorbs that image and incorporates it into your life. This process encourages you to enjoy a new thought, a new attitude, or a new behavior.

Simply sit back and relax. If you are more comfortable on a bed, that's just fine. Don't worry if you fall asleep. As you read this chapter, you may decide to take breaks here and there by closing your eyes and picturing in your mind the scenes you're reading about.

Find a quiet place where you will not be disturbed. A place where there is no phone, no Blackberry—just you.

This journey takes you along a path and that path permits you to feel good—really good—calm and comfortable, rested and relaxed. You will enjoy this wonderful mind/body experience.

1. *Take a deep breath.* Give yourself permission to feel your body slowing down. Good. Feel your body relaxing. You are experiencing a lovely heavy feeling. A feeling of relief. You are feeling slowed down. Your hands and feet are so heavy and so quiet. Your entire body is quiet.
2. *Slow down your mind.* Your mind is quiet. Your thoughts are slowing down. Give yourself permission to feel your mind relaxing. Good. You are reading these words and feeling very relaxed.
3. *Let the heavy feeling surround you.* Imagine that you are walking down a path. There is grass on both sides of you—see it in your mind. And then you'll see some trees, some bushes, and some beautiful greenery.

4. *Pause from reading.* Allow yourself to visualize this scene for a couple of minutes.

5. *Resume reading.* You are following the right path—this is where you should be—where you belong. Look up and see the blue sky—there's a cloud drifting by. See the gorgeous sun. Feel the warmth of the sun.

   Listen carefully and perhaps you will hear some birds, and there are other comforting sounds of nature, too.

   Take a deep breath and smell the sweet air.

   Watch yourself, in your mind, as you walk. Keep walking. Notice the green grass and now look over there and you'll see some bright flowers—colorful and beautiful.

   Watch yourself as you continue walking.

   You are comfortable.

   You are content. You are at peace.

   At peace with the universe. At peace with yourself.

6. *Pause again, close your eyes and visualize this comforting scene, with you in it, for a couple of minutes.*

7. *Open your eyes and slowly resume reading.* As you continue strolling, your burdens lift. Please give yourself permission to enjoy yourself on this walk. Yes, you may enjoy yourself. You can enjoy yourself. You should enjoy yourself. It is good for you to enjoy yourself.

   Stop for a moment and notice the beauty all around you.

   Take a deep breath and smell the aromas of nature.

   Listen, and hear the sweet sounds of the outdoors.

   Notice the beauty of nature. See the colorful flowers.

   You will always have nature near you. You will always have the ability to be near beauty . . . and then to feel peaceful.

   Whenever you need to improve your mood, you can visualize yourself on this path.

   This is a wonderful path that you are on. Allow yourself to feel safe and secure, calm and comfortable. You are well protected. The warmth of the sun comforts you. The flowers bring joy to your heart.

   You continue to walk. You are enjoying yourself. Your mind and body are at peace.

You are becoming calmer and calmer. Your mind is healing. Your mind is healing your body.

You can create this feeling of peacefulness whenever you need to, simply by imagining your path. The path will lead you to contentment.

Continue to enjoy your walk and then pause whenever you wish. Whenever you are ready just continue reading and begin to stroll around again. Stroll for as long you'd like. Walk here, walk there, smell the flowers.

Feel the calmness surrounding you. You are enjoying yourself.

Notice a beautiful flower. There is one particular flower that is outstanding. The image of that beautiful flower will remain in your mind. Whenever you see that flower in your mind, you will immediately come into this state of serenity, of peacefulness, of quiet.

Stay on the path as long as you'd like. Remain with your flower as long as you'd like. If you wish to stop reading this and close your eyes and see your flower, then go right ahead and do so.

You are feeling safe and secure, calm and comfortable. Good. Enjoy the feelings of security . . . of comfort. You deserve these good feelings.

Now you know that you can feel good. You can escape from the everyday pressures. Good for you.

Look at your flower. This is a delightful flower. You've been on a delightful walk.

Then, whenever you feel ready, you may begin to retrace your steps and come back to the beginning of the path. When you are back at the beginning of the path, you will slowly, at your own pace, begin to return your ordinary feelings back to your mind and return your ordinary feelings back to your body.

Please take your time. We have plenty of time. You may continue walking for as long you like. Then when you are ready, you will return to your starting point on the path.

Allow your hands and feet to come back to regular. The heaviness throughout your body will slowly diminish. Take your time, you have plenty of time.

You may wish to stretch out, sit up, and come back to regular. Good. You did a good job.

Every good feeling you experienced on this path will stay with you. Every good feeling you experienced is a feeling that you produced. All the good, calm, restful feelings that you experienced while reading this exercise originated within you. These feelings are yours. You have the ability to create them whenever you need them.

Read these words whenever you would like to bring back the wonderful feelings of peacefulness and calmness . . . the wonderful feelings of serenity . . . solace.

Notice that you are emerging from your walk on the path with feelings of contentment.

Whenever you want to recreate these feelings simply picture the path in your mind and then in your mind see yourself walking.

Take a deep breath. Sit up and stretch out. Now you are alert and you are ready to resume your life. Lucky you. You are content. You can handle your life with ease and with pleasure. You did a good job on this path and with your flower. Congratulations.

If you'd like, you can order a recording, on a CD, of this walk in the park along with other soothing and healing visualizations that I've created specifically for people going through bereavement. Just click on www .solaceafteradeath.com.

CHAPTER 8

Your Future

Your journey through bereavement is ending and you are focusing on your future. Good for you!

From now on:

- *You will figure out how to proceed ahead with your life.* Whenever life's unfairness smacks you in the face you won't ask, "why?," but instead you will ask, "now what?" and you'll plan a plan. Perhaps you'll be like Joe, who upon being bereaved decided that whenever someone asked him to join them for any activity, he would say "yes." Or maybe you'll be like Marie, who felt she needed more religion in her life after the loss of her brother. She continues to go to Mass every day, volunteers for many church committees, and schedules regular visits with her parish priest.
- *You will figure out how to keep alive the values of the person you loved.* Perhaps you'll be like Marty, who endowed a fund in his wife's name. His wife loved theater and Marty made it possible for poor high school students, who couldn't afford Broadway prices, to be his guests at matinees. Or maybe you'll be like Ruth. "What do you do when you have a twenty-year-old daughter who is gone in an instant? You don't just put a plaque on the wall," said Ruth Schulman. Her daughter, Adina Schulman, was a New Jersey college student when she had a sudden, severe headache, fell to the floor, and died. In Adina's

memory, her mother established a fund to help young people accomplish projects in the areas of interest to Adina, which were civil rights and peace.

• *You will figure out how to keep alive some habits of the person you loved.* Sam loved to whistle and now his older brother has become a whistler. Ellie always flossed her teeth after a meal, even in a restaurant. Her daughter thought that was rude and gross. But that daughter now does the very same thing. Allison's sister-in-law used the phrase "okeydokey." Allison didn't want that expression to be gone from family life, so now she says it. Eleanor loved to iron and went to work with crisp shirts and pleated slacks. Now her husband irons all his shirts. He used to show up at work a bit wrinkled.

• *You will remember that your experience has made you a specialist in grief.* Perhaps you'll be like Rita, who upon hearing about a young woman whose mother just died, immediately reached out to her. Rita shared her story about her own mother's death and her reactions to it. She knew what to say; she knew how to console the young woman. You, too, can console another bereaved person—others will benefit from your expertise and your experience. Or maybe you'll be like Harry, who was overwhelmed when his wife died but knew that keeping up his weekly poker game with old friends would be good for his mental health. Eventually, Harry sought out newly widowed men and invited them to his game. To this day, Harry's buddies know that sometimes he will show up with several guys in tow. Expanding a widower's social network is a step toward recovery from bereavement.

• *You will recognize a part of your personality—a strength—that you were unaware of.* You will use this strength to your advantage. This is your opportunity to recognize power and talent you never knew you had. In 2001, when Seth and Sherri Mandell's thirteen-year-old son was murdered by terrorists, the Mandells established a foundation in memory of Koby, their son. Among the missions of the foundation is to provide nurturing and bereavement care for mothers of children murdered by terrorists.

You have the capacity to adapt to your new circumstance. You are psychologically resilient. Gradually, you will change your self-image and self-definition to reflect the life circumstance that exists for you today. Your life is manageable. You can do it.

Although some pain may occasionally surface, suffering because of that pain is optional. Don't take that option.

REINVENTION

Certainly there is nothing good about the death or about your grief and mourning, yet there is a bonus to completing bereavement. The completion of bereavement provides you the opportunity to try out new ways of being.

When you are in a close and loving relationship, you find a way to behave that enhances that relationship. Now, you can try out different behaviors, different ideas. If you were the strong one in the relationship and could never show any weakness, now you have a chance to reveal some of your uncertainties. If you were the dependent one who needed advice and guidance about everything, now you have the chance to make your own decisions.

In my practice I've seen meek, dowdy wives transformed into glamorous widows. I've seen elderly conservative executives take flying lessons, and I've seen a young mother go back to school and become a doctor in the hope of curing the illness from which her son died.

Frank, a widower who never stepped into the kitchen when his wife was alive, actually took baking lessons and now is considering a second career in the catering business. Frank explained:

> "Mary was a fabulous cook and baker. I wouldn't want to get in her way and I figured I could never prepare anything as good as she did, anyway. So, when she was alive I never tried. That's all changed now. It makes me feel closer to her when I'm in the kitchen using her utensils, and don't use my last name if you put this in your book, but sometimes when I am especially lonely I put on Mary's apron when I bake."

If you played the docile partner because your loved one needed to be bossy, here's your chance to become more assertive. If you played the capable expert because your partner was insecure and needed constant reassurance, this is your chance to be humble and become open to new experiences.

Nanette always engaged in battles with her mom. Nanette was known to be a difficult young woman. After her mother died, the difficult young woman changed. She actually came in for a consultation with me because she thought there was something wrong—she was now easy to get along with. She didn't pick fights with coworkers. She didn't argue with her brother. She was no longer irritable on the subway. Nanette couldn't understand what was happening to her—she was becoming a nice person.

Nanette was relieved when I explained that because her mom was no longer with her, she did not need to perpetuate the role of adversary. For some reason, going back decades, Nanette and her mom were comfortable snapping at each other. It was the way in which they showed their love for one another. It was a familiar pattern that they each perpetuated. But, the negativity carried over into other parts of Nanette's life. She was in the habit of fighting and that habit entered all her relationships. Her mom's death permitted her to relate to others in a new and different fashion. Nanette stopped fighting when her mother died.

Was your loved one difficult to get along with? Many people find that the best way to enjoy a good relationship with a difficult person is to be compliant. It is sometimes easier to say, "Yes, dear," than to have constant arguments. If you've always been compliant, this is your opportunity to assert yourself.

Some people, when in a relationship that threatens to smother them, become defiant. It is sometimes less scary to simply rebel than to follow all the orders that a loved one is dishing out. If you've been constantly rebellious or defiant, here's your chance to have a calmer lifestyle. You no longer need to defend yourself; now you can take it easy.

Jeanne Safer, a psychotherapist, is the author of *Death Benefits: How Losing a Parent Can Change an Adult's Life—For the Better*. While Safer acknowledges the deep pain and sorrow experienced after the death of a parent, she goes on to address those adults who wish to transform themselves in some significant ways. Safer believes that a parental death can jump-start that process. Safer's book will be useful to you if your deceased parent was not your dear friend or confidante, or if your parent's presence prevented you from being all you could be. Safer teaches techniques for emotional growth especially geared for those whose relationships with their beloved parents may have been somewhat strained.

If you were successful in your relationship with your loved one, it was because you knew what that person needed from you. That was a good thing. That's what makes relationships work. Now, please feel free to use this opportunity to bring out a part of you that might have been hidden because it would not have been good for the relationship. You can alter your old ways of doing things if you are so inclined.

Mike came to see me after his son died. Mike's son had a debilitating muscle disease and for many years Mike and his wife devoted themselves to the care of their child. Mike explained:

"Now that Chris is gone I don't need to be cautious. For years, I wouldn't allow myself to play in my company's softball league or to go hiking with my buddies. I feared if I had even a slight injury I wouldn't be able to lift Chris, and he was too heavy for Vera, my wife, to lift. But now I can afford to take a risk. I'm going hunting in November. And I'll be weight lifting at the gym, too. Lifting Chris gave me muscles and I want to keep them. Looking at my muscles helps me keep a picture of Chris in my mind. He gave me those muscles so I don't want to lose them. My sisters and my brother cracked up laughing when I told them about going to the gym. I guess I'm not that type of a guy."

You have survived bereavement, so you know that you have strengths and assets. You can undertake new activities and succeed at them. So acknowledge your resourcefulness, and continue to master new skills.

Many people like the idea of having an event to honor the deceased. If you decide to publicly celebrate the life of your beloved, you will use your newfound strengths to do so. Maybe you'll sponsor a lecture about his favorite topic, or perhaps a concert of her favorite songs. You can accomplish this goal, if you wish, using your recently demonstrated powerfulness. Look at what you've endured and rejoice that you are here to tell the tale. You are capable and you are competent. Your self-respect is soaring. You have survived quite an ordeal.

Selma mastered a new skill right after her husband died. When Leo died, his wife, Selma, knew that although fame and fortune eluded him, Leo had enjoyed good relationships with his customers. He ran the fruit department in the neighborhood supermarket. Selma got permission from the store manager to put a small sign up near the watermelons. The sign told of Leo's death from a sudden heart attack and invited everyone to a short memorial service to be held at the town park that Sunday. Thirty-five people showed up, and most got up to speak. They told of Leo's kindness and helpfulness. One customer mentioned that Leo offered her son and daughter some grapes and even washed them for the kids. Some people noted that Leo learned their preferences such as what type of lettuce or which apples were favorites. Leo's boss told of Leo's good work ethic and loyalty, and then surprised the group by treating everyone to fresh fruit.

Selma told me: "Dr. Roberta, this was my proudest moment. I only wish Leo was there to see me. I was in charge and I made all the arrangements. I never did anything like this in my life. I shocked myself. He was truly honored."

Reinvention is not for everyone. Most mourners are just fine with their life and their lifestyle. Use good judgment, and know what should be changed and what should be left alone.

CONCLUSION

As you reenter life, you'll realize that you live but once and this is not a dress rehearsal. This is it. To honor the memory of your loved one, give yourself permission to experience happiness amid your sadness.

PLAYWRIGHT JOANNE KOCH'S STORY

Why don't I grieve? The question reminds me of Linda Loman at the end of *Death of a Salesman* telling Willy at his grave that she can't cry. In my case, I was able to cry when my mother, Ceil Eidelsheim Schapiro, died. But I didn't feel intense grief and am not sure I went through a "normal" mourning period. Is that because for me, she never died? I don't mean anything creepy about that. I just mean, for me she is such a palpable force in my life every day, I don't feel she's gone. I look at her life and ask, why this absence of grief? Why didn't her death bring about years of mourning?

Here's one source of my strength. Mom shared her own early life with me so completely when I was growing up, that I experienced vicariously the challenges and triumphs of her childhood and youth, absorbing some of her unique mixture of grit and humor, unflinching realism and zesty optimism. That helped me weather the storm and stress of my own adolescence, but much later it helped me cope with the painful prospect of life without Mom. She told me in vivid detail how, starting at age 5, she became her older sister's protector because that sister, Henrietta, was crippled by polio; how at age 15 when her father lost his job, she left high school, donned lipstick and cheap high heels and landed the secretarial position that made her the sole breadwinner for her family through the worst years of the Depression. These stories were like inoculations against my own hard times and losses ahead, including the loss of my mother.

Mom modeled for me every stage of adult life—the supportive parent to my brother and myself, the loving and capable wife, the affectionate grandmother for my brother's and my children, the helpmate for my dad when a stroke forced him to abruptly leave his still thriving medical career, and then again when another left him wheelchair-bound.

After Dad died, she was the attractive widow who resisted meeting anyone for ten years. Then, in her late eighties, came a sudden and totally uncharacteristic period of depression. When I convinced her, after several months of debilitating sadness, to move to a small, cozy, nearby assisted living facility, she returned to the cheerful, curious Ceil I had known and loved. And then an incredible thing happened. Ceil, age 88, and Lou, another resident in the facility, age 92, fell in love. For five years, they had a carefree romance that made every day for them an adventure.

So even in what sociologists call "old-old age," Ceil lived life to the fullest. She had the almost giddy pleasure of discovering another totally unexpected soul mate when she had forgotten that such feelings were still possible.

In the last three months of her life, when a narrowing heart valve was literally taking her breath away, Ceil made the choice to say good-bye to the life she had enthusiastically lived. She told me, "I had a good life. I'm satisfied to end it now."

Did I cry—yes. Do I wish she were still here—yes. Do I think of her every day and often dream she is here—yes, yes, yes.

But I don't feel grief. I'm not mournful. I don't think Ceil did one single thing in her life that she regretted, and she did so much she could celebrate. No—the thought of her life simply fills me with joy.

I was fortunate to experience a long, unambiguous yet realistic relationship with my mother. When I have to go, may it be a good-bye with no regrets and a legacy for my children of life lived to its fullest. Perhaps then, they will be spared the need to spend years grieving.

Take pride in your coping ability. You'll be amazed at your adjustment. Become aware of your progress in the way you feel and in the way you think. You are finding your way through grief. You will live. You will live well. You will have a good life.

To help you proceed ahead in your life think about how you would like to be remembered when you die. Yes, you want to be remembered for accomplishments and successes. But also think about relationships and ways that you can show that you are kind and thoughtful. Think about making the world a better place because of one or two little things you might do. You know what is important. Acts of kindness go a long way. Character counts.

I wish your days to be filled with kindness and goodness and many reasons to smile. I wish your nights to be filled with secure sleep and sweet peace. I hope you follow a life-affirming path and I wish you a fine life ahead, full of good memories and laughter and love.

This is Dr. Roberta saying bye for now. It has been an honor to share information with you. You are invited to stay in touch with me at www .solaceafterdeath.com.

Appendix

Books can help. However, you need to be selective. Some books will appeal to you and others will not. Wendy Schoenbach, in her unpublished memoir, wrote about her experience with *bibliotherapy*. Bibliotherapy is the use of reading to create a change, for the better, in your life. Schoenbach said, "Over the years, since my father's death, I have tried getting comfort from books. But the confidence and positive attitudes of the authors, usually mental health professionals, gave an impression of smugness that repelled me."

The books I've listed here will not repel you. They are useful, and I encourage you to read at least one and then refer to this list months and even years from now. I've divided the books into sections.

The books in the following section are supportive and inspirational. They will help you get through the dark days of grief:

Canfield, Jack, and Mark Victor Hansen, comp. *Chicken Soup for the Grieving Soul: Stories About Life, Death, and Overcoming the Loss of a Loved One.* Deerfield Beach, FL: Health Communications, 2003.
This book, part of a best-selling series, features a collection of stories by people who have lost loved ones. The different experiences featured provide support and encouragement to those grieving a loss.

Frankl, Viktor E. *Man's Search for Meaning.* Boston: Beacon Press, 2006.

Doctor Frankl was an Austrian neurologist and psychiatrist, as well as a Holocaust survivor. In the first half of this book, he writes about his struggle to find reasons to live during the five years he was imprisoned in concentration camps. In the second half of the book, he discusses the psychotherapeutic approach that he pioneered, based on the belief that man is driven by his search to find meaning. This book is written in layman's language and encourages you to derive comfort from life's hardships while gaining insight into the meaning of life.

Guntzelman, Ph.D., Joan. *God Knows You're Grieving: Things to Do to Help You Through.* Notre Dame, IN: Sorin Books, 2001.
Guntzelman—a writer, professor, and therapist—offers comfort and encouragement through shared stories, thoughtful insights, prayers, and practical suggestions for healing.

Hickman, Martha Whitmore. *Healing After Loss: Daily Meditations for Working Through Grief.* New York: Avon Books, 1994.
Hickman, the author of more than twenty books for adults and children, has compiled 365 meditations—one for each day of the year. Each page contains an inspirational quote and thoughts for healing.

Kumar, Ph.D., Sameet M. *Grieving Mindfully: A Compassionate and Spiritual Guide to Coping with Loss.* Oakland, CA: New Harbinger Publications, 2005.
Dr. Kumar, a psychologist at the Mount Sinai Comprehensive Cancer Center and an expert in Buddhist meditation, combines psychology and Buddhism to help readers cope with their grief. He offers mindful exercises that encourage acceptance of grief as well as strategies for making life more meaningful.

Kushner, Harold S. *When Bad Things Happen to Good People.* New York: Schocken Books, 1989.
Kushner, a Conservative rabbi, wrote this book in reaction to his son's death at age 14. This book, a *New York Times* best seller, offers understanding, strength, and hope.

Noel, Brook, and Pamela D. Blair, Ph.D. *I Wasn't Ready to Say Goodbye: Surviving, Coping, and Healing After the Sudden Death of a Loved One.* Naperville, IL: Sourcebooks, Inc., 2008.
Brook, the author of nineteen books on grief, bereavement, and life management, teams with Blair, a therapist and educator, to review the different types of sudden loss. The authors combine their personal experiences with loss with the

experiences of others who have faced unexpected deaths caused by a variety of situations. This book includes practical advice and specific actions to take to help with both short- and long-term healing.

Radziwill, Carole. *What Remains: A Memoir of Fate, Friendship, and Love.* New York: Scribner, 2005.
This is the best-selling memoir of a Kennedy family member who suffered the loss of her husband and two best friends within three weeks of each other. Radziwill recounts her life from working-class girl to award-winning television producer and member of the Kennedy family. She discusses her marriage, the importance of friendship, and how she found the strength to survive multiple losses. This would be a heartbreaking story even if it were not written by the widow of Anthony Radziwill, a nephew of Jacqueline Kennedy Onassis. The author describes her husband's diagnosis and eventual death from cancer, as well as her shock and sorrow when her dear friend, Carolyn Bessette Kennedy, was killed along with her husband, John F. Kennedy Jr., in a plane crash.

Rando, Ph.D., Therese A. *How to Go On Living When Someone You Love Dies.* New York: Bantam Books, 1991.
Bereavement specialist and author Dr. Rando explains that each person's response to loss is different and then guides readers to find their best way to grieve.

Sheehy, Gail. *Middletown, America: One Town's Passage from Trauma to Hope.* New York: Random House, 2003.
Best-selling author Sheehy spent almost two years observing the reactions of residents in this New Jersey town that lost fifty people from the 9/11 terror attacks. Sheehy conducted more than nine hundred interviews and reports it all. She concentrates, though, on four moms whose sorrow and anger turned them into political activists. You will read inspiring accounts of resilient preschool children, courageous parents, and widows and widowers who learn to love again.

Temes, Peter S. *The Power of Purpose: Living Well by Doing Good.* New York: Harmony, 2006.
Temes, founder of the ILO Institute, an organization that researches innovation for multi-billion-dollar corporations, explores the best way to lead a meaningful life. He draws on the wisdom of a wide range of people from Aristotle to Michael Jordan and identifies helping others as the path toward happiness and success.

Viorst, Judith. *Necessary Losses: The Loves, Illusions, Dependencies, and Impossible Expectations That All of Us Have to Give Up in Order to Grow.* New York: Simon and Schuster, 1986.

Best-selling poet and author Viorst offers her theory that in every stage of life there are losses to endure that are necessary in order to grow. She takes the reader from the loss of a mother's protection to the loss of youth and expectations to the death of loved ones. Viorst uses her studies and work in the field of psychoanalysis, as well as literature and a multitude of interviews, to support her belief that these losses are inevitable and critical. Viorst maintains that coping with these losses helps develop a strong sense of self.

The following books will help you cope with the aftermath of a suicide:

Cobain, Beverly, and Jean Larch. *Dying to Be Free: A Healing Guide for Families After a Suicide.* Center City, MN: Hazelden Publishing and Educational Services, 2006.

This book addresses the shame, silence, and stigma surrounding suicide. Author Cobain is a relative of Nirvana singer Kurt Cobain, who committed suicide in 1994. She recounts her story as well as the stories of many others who have lost a family member to suicide. Larch, a suicide counselor, adds her advice on how to handle the confusion, fear, and sometimes guilt that family members may experience when a loved one commits suicide.

Collins, Judy. *The Seven T's: Finding Hope and Healing in the Wake of Tragedy.* New York: Jeremy P. Tarcher Penguin, 2007.

Singer/songwriter Collins, whose son committed suicide in 1992, outlines a seven-step approach toward coping with tragedy and loss. Collins spoke with hundreds of people who grieved the death of a loved one in order to develop this step-by-step method of healing. This book will be useful even if your loved one did not die from suicide.

Fine, Carla. *No Time to Say Goodbye: Surviving the Suicide of a Loved One.* New York: Doubleday, 1997.

Fine, whose previous book was about being a doctor's wife, lost her husband to suicide and wrote this book to help others in her situation. She consulted experts and interviewed survivors in order to create this comprehensive manual to guide suicide survivors though their grief. This book offers comfort and guidance if you are experiencing the complex emotions and issues often associated with suicide.

The following books are written especially for men:

Chethik, Neil. *FatherLoss: How Sons of All Ages Come to Terms with the Deaths of Their Dads.* New York: Hyperion, 2001.
This book, based on a survey of three hundred men and interviews with seventy others, explores the grieving process men go through at different ages. It covers many areas related to men and loss and includes a description of four specific styles of grieving.

Lund, Ph.D., Dale A., ed. *Men Coping with Grief.* Amityville, NY: Baywood Publishing Company, 2000.
Dr. Lund, an author and researcher, compiled this volume that features a diverse group of authors who share their professional and personal knowledge about how men grieve.

The following books are written for adults who lose a parent:

Brooks, Jane. *Midlife Orphan: Facing Life's Changes Now That Your Parents Are Gone.* New York: Berkley Trade, 1999.
The author, a writer and teacher, explores the effects of losing your parents when you are a grown-up. She discusses changes in self-image, unresolved feelings, inheritance, and the shifting of roles.

Gilbert, Allison, and Christina Baker Kline, eds. *Always Too Soon: Voices of Support for Those Who Have Lost Both Parents.* Emeryville, CA: Seal Press, 2006.
CNN producer Gilbert compiled this collection of interviews with famous people who have lost both parents. You will read about Geraldine Ferraro, Ice T, and Yogi Berra, among others. Anyone who has lost one or both parents will relate to these personal stories of grief for a parent.

Safer, Jeanne. *Death Benefits: How Losing a Parent Can Change an Adult's Life—For the Better.* New York: Basic Books, 2008.
Written for grieving adult children of critical or rejecting parents, psychologist Safer offers the view that losing such a parent can give the grieving adult child the chance to change for the better. Based on her own experience and those of sixty patients and interviewees, Safer outlines helpful exercises for healing the emotional wounds inflicted by dysfunctional parents. She teaches the reader how to find a sense of self without feelings of guilt.

Secunda, Victoria. *Losing Your Parents, Finding Your Self: The Defining Turning Point of Adult Life.* New York: Hyperion, 2000.

Secunda—an award-winning author, journalist, and lecturer—offers this compilation of her survey of ninety-four people, each of whom has lost parents as adults. She illustrates the various ways growth can occur from parental loss. She talks about giving up one's identity as a child and more fully embracing an adult self though other relationships.

The following books are for widows and widowers:

Brothers, Dr. Joyce. *Widowed.* New York: Simon and Schuster, 1990.
This famous author/psychologist writes about her personal journey through bereavement when her beloved husband of many years died of cancer. Dr. Brothers describes feelings and situations that other widows will relate to. She offers hope and support by sharing how she found strength, amid much struggle, and put her life back together.

Didion, Joan. *The Year of Magical Thinking.* New York: Knopf, 2005.
Well-known author Didion wrote this memoir about her husband's death at the time when their only daughter was hospitalized and in a coma. Didion chronicles how she struggled to keep her sanity during this challenging time. Because she is an excellent writer, her words are sharp and her images insightful. The tone of this book is immediate and truthful; the reader is right there with Didion on every page. This book became a play in 2007 starring Vanessa Redgrave.

Feinberg, Linda Sones. *I'm Grieving as Fast as I Can.* Far Hills, NJ: New Horizon Press, 1994.
This book is particularly geared to the young widow or widower. The author tells about the experiences of the many young widows and widowers with whom she has worked, and how they coped with the untimely death of a spouse. This book includes advice on how to talk to young children experiencing the death of a parent, dealing with in-laws, and going back to work.

Steen, Joanne M., and M. Regina Asaro. *Military Widow: A Survival Guide.* Annapolis, MD: U.S. Naval Institute Press, 2006.
Steen, a counselor and widow of a naval aviator, teams with psychiatric nurse and crisis responder Asaro in this guide for the military widow. This book addresses the unique and complex issues arising from the death of a spouse in the military. It includes the stories of other military widows and features short, easy-to-read chapters that also will be useful to other family members, friends, and military professionals.

The following books are written specifically for parents, and in one case, grandparents, who have suffered the loss of a child:

Finkbeiner, Ann K. *After the Death of a Child: Living with Loss Through the Years*. New York: Free Press, 1996.
Finkbeiner, a writer whose only child died at eighteen, focuses on the long-term effects on parents of a child's death. She interviewed and met with thirty parents, all of whom had lost a child at least five years prior. Topics covered include the disorientation parents experience, the ongoing grief they feel, and the various coping mechanisms they can utilize.

Hood, Ann. *Comfort: A Journey Through Grief*. New York: W. W. Norton, 2008.
This is a memoir about the sudden death of the author's five-year-old daughter. Hood, a successful writer and novelist, tells her story of loss, surviving grief, and ultimately finding hope.

Mandell, Sherri. *The Blessing of a Broken Heart*. New Milford, CT: Toby Press, 2003.
This is the memoir of a mother who survived the murder of her thirteen-year-old son. Mandell, an American-born writer living in Israel, talks about her path toward healing after her eldest son was killed by terrorists while on a hike with his friend. She discusses the role her Jewish faith played in helping her mourn and how she was able to transform her grief into compassion by helping others who, too, lost a loved one to terrorism.

Marx, Robert J., and Susan Wengerhoff Davidson. *Facing the Ultimate Loss: Coping with the Death of a Child*. Fredonia, WI: Champion Press Ltd., 2003.
A rabbi and a grief therapist, both of whom lost a child, team up to offer guidelines that can help grieving parents cope with their overwhelming feelings. They acknowledge that people mourn and deal with grief in many different ways and offer a path toward continuing the journey of living. This book will be useful to professionals or anyone close to bereaved parents.

Redfern, Suzanne, and Susan K. Gilbert. *The Grieving Garden: Living with the Death of a Child*. Charlottesville, VA: Hampton Roads Publishing Company, 2008.
Redfern and Gilbert, who both lost daughters, wrote this book because they didn't find the comfort they were looking for in the existing literature on child loss. Along with twenty other grieving parents, they share their experience and offer practical guidance on handling specific challenges. The book is organized into twenty-four issues that parents face. The reader is presented with a variety of perspectives, backgrounds, and circumstances.

Reed, Mary Lou. *Grandparents Cry Twice: Help for Bereaved Grandparents*. Amityville, NY: Baywood Publishing Company, 2000.

The author, a nurse who became a grief counselor after the death of her grandson, wrote this book to help other grandparents cope with dual sorrow— grieving the loss of the grandchild and feeling the parent's pain as well. The book includes advice from other grieving grandparents and offers suggestions for memorials and personal rituals that can help all family members cope with their pain.

The following books are written for children and/or teens who are bereaved:

Bunting, Eve, and Ronald Himler, illustrator. *Rudi's Pond*. New York: Clarion Books, 1999.

This is a picture book for children five to eight years old by prolific author Eve Bunting. It is based on a true story about the death of a little boy and how his friends and classmates remember him. This story can offer comfort to other children who have suffered a similar loss.

Gootman, Marilyn E. *When a Friend Dies: A Book for Teens About Grieving and Healing*. Minneapolis, MN: Free Spirit Publishing, 1994.

This is a brief guide to help teens and young adults cope with the loss of a friend. It offers simple, practical advice on handling feelings as well as dealing with difficult situations.

Temes, Ph.D., Roberta, and Kim Carlisle, illustrator. *The Empty Place: A Child's Guide Through Grief*. Far Hills, NJ: New Horizon Press, 1992.

I wrote this book to help children age 4 through 10, or even older, cope and heal from the death of a loved one. The story is about a nine-year-old boy who is confused, angry, fearful, and guilty after the death of his sister. The book provides an example of a young boy using a journal to get some mastery over his feelings. Interestingly, this book was recently translated into Chinese to be used for survivors of the 2008 Sichuan earthquake.

Wolfelt, Ph.D., Alan. *Healing A Teen's Grieving Heart: 100 Practical Ideas*. Fort Collins, CO: Companion Press, 2001.

This practical guide encourages teens to embrace their loss and warns them about dangerous ways of escaping in order to avoid pain. Dr. Wolfert presents several ideas for releasing grief in healthy, positive ways.

The following books are for adults who are helping children proceed through grief:

Emswiler, Mary Ann, and James P. Emswiler. *Guiding Your Child Through Grief.* New York: Bantam, 2000.
The authors, founders of the program for grieving children at the New England Center for Loss and Transition, offer parents advice on helping children grieve the loss of a loved one. This book includes tips on how to talk to children of different ages and suggests ways to talk about different kinds of death. It includes tips for school personnel and also has a suggested reading list for all ages, through the teen years.

Lewis, Paddy Greenwall, and Jessica G. Lippman. *Helping Children Cope with the Death of a Parent: A Guide for the First Year.* Westport, CT: Praeger Publishers, 2004.
Child psychologists Lewis and Lippman offer their shared experience of counseling children who have lost their parents. This book offers practical methods for dealing with the particularly difficult first year after loss. It includes stories of some of the children whom they have helped.

The next book is an important book, yet it defies being categorized into any of the previous areas:

DeVita-Raeburn, Elizabeth. *The Empty Room: Surviving the Loss of a Brother or Sister at Any Age.* New York: Scribner, 2004.
Raeburn, a science journalist who lost her older brother when she was six, recounts her life with him and the unique challenges she faced in dealing with his death. She discusses her interviews with seventy-seven people who lost siblings and offers tools for coping with this type of loss. This is an important book. Many psychologists and grief therapists believe that sibling death is not given enough attention.

Please read. You will benefit.

Bibliography
by Chapter

CHAPTER ONE

Brothers, Joyce. *Widowed*. New York: Simon and Schuster, 1990.

Etzioni, Amitai. "Good Grief." *New York Times*, October 7, 2006.

Gaylin, Willard. *New York Times* interview with Daniel Goleman, October 5, 1985.

Hayes, Helen. *On Reflection*. New York: M. Evans & Co., 1968.

Lewis, C. S. *A Grief Observed*. San Francisco: Harper San Francisco, 2001.

Shakespeare, Wm., et al. *King Henry VI*, Act I, Scene 1, in *The Oxford Shakespeare, Complete Works*. 2nd ed. New York: Oxford University Press, 2005.

CHAPTER TWO

Hood, Ann. *Comfort: A Journey Through Grief*. New York: W. W. Norton, 2008.

Maimonides, Moses. *The Guide of the Perplexed*. Chaim Rabin, trans. Indianapolis, IN: Hackett Publishing, 1995.

O'Connor, Mary-Francis. "Craving Love?" *Neuroimage*, 42, no. 2 (2008): 969–972.

CHAPTER THREE

Arcana, Judith. "Dead Young Mother." 2008.

Collins, Billy. Interview with Terry Gross on NPR, 2001.

Didion, Joan. *The Year of Magical Thinking.* New York: Knopf, 2005.

Mandell, Sherry "Transforming Grief into Action." *Jewish Woman.* (Fall 2003).

CHAPTER FOUR

Attenborough, Lord Richard. *The Daily Mail.* London, England, December 24, 2007.

Compassionate Friends. *Mission Statement,* www.compassionatefriends.org.

Donnelly, Katherine Fair. *Recovering from the Loss of a Child.* New York: Macmillan Publishers, 1982.

Oliveri, Terry. "Grief Groups on the Internet." *Bereavement Care* 22, no. 3 (2003): 39–40.

Rehm, Nancy. Letter to the Editor. *New York Times,* March 25, 2008.

CHAPTER FIVE

Brody, Jane E. "Alternatives for the Final Disposition." Personal Health column. *New York Times,* April 15, 2008.

Kennedy, Rose Fitzgerald. *Times to Remember.* Garden City, NY: Doubleday & Co., 1974.

Staples, Brent. *Parallel Time: Growing Up in Black and White.* New York: Pantheon Books, 1994.

CHAPTER SIX

Lincoln, Abraham. *Speeches and Writings 1859–1865.* Don Edward Fehrenbacher, annotations. New York: Literary Classics of the United States, 1989.

Winerip, Michael. "Helping Hand for Children Mourning Death of Loved One." Parenting column. *New York Times,* October 28, 2007.

CHAPTER EIGHT

Koch, Joanne. *Why I Don't Grieve.* Unpublished. 2008.

Safer, Jeanne. *Death Benefits: How Losing a Parent Can Change an Adult's Life—For the Better.* New York: Basic Books, 2008.

Index

functioning, automatic, 10
funeral director, 69–70
funerals, 89–94
future, 21
  as focus, 121–128

Gaylin, Willard, 16
ghosts, 31
Gifts of Grief (YouTube video), 87–88
God, 36
Goldman, Carl, 69
Good Grief Camps, 83
gravestone, 97
Greece, 95
green burials, 91
grief, 5
  anticipatory, 14–15
  complicated, 26–28, 64
  cumulative, 26
  disenfranchised, 58–61
  style, 2–3
Grief, Australia, 81–82
Grief Blog, 85
grief chat room, 75–76
Grief Matters for Children, 77
Grief Recovery Institute, 80
GriefNet, 79
Grief's Journey, 81
guided imagery, 117–120
guilt, 13
gun control, 42

habits, 31
hallucinations, 30–31
Hammer, Kim, 82
Hayes, Helen, 15
help for yourself, 113–120
  tapping cure, 113–117
  visualizations, 117–120
help from others
  bereavement counselors, 64–68
  bereavement groups, 55–64
  for children, 103–111
  family and friends, 70–72

financial assistants, 73–74
functions, 23
funeral director, 69–70
Internet resources, 74–88
response to, 10
Hindus, 95–96
holidays, 99
Hood, Ann, *Comfort*, 30
hope, loss of, 14
Hospice International, 82
Hospice Net, 79
hospitals, care for family, 61
husband, death of, 61

immune system, stress and, 34
India, 95–96
Internet resources, 74–88
  blogs, 84–86
  online support groups, 75–76
  websites, 76–84
  YouTube, 86–88
isolation, avoiding, 40

James, John W., 80
Japan, 95
Jewish mourners
  Kaddish, 63–64
  shivah, 94
journal entries, 47
justice, 62

Kaddish, 63–64
Kennedy, Rose Fitzgerald, 99
Koch, Joanne, 126–128
Korea, 96
Kübler-Ross, Elizabeth, *On Death and Dying*, 18–19

Lakota tribe of Native Americans, 96
laughter, 35
leaders, of bereavement groups, 56
learning, as therapy, 51
Legacy.com, 77
Lennon, John, 50